Hurt Used To Live Here

Joyce Reed

www.iamURvoice.com

DEDICATION

To all the women and men that are carrying around the shame, guilt, the embarrassment of being afraid of what they been through and endure. I am UR voice and you are not alone. I pray that after you read my story it will give you the strength and courage to speak out and let UR voice be heard. Release that weight off of your shoulders.

My #1 Boo in ATL, you did that Boo and I love you forever

Love

Joyce Ren

Hurt Used To Live Here By Joyce Reed

Edited by Alicia Shines and Dennis Moore
Book Servicing by B.O.S.S. Publishing ~~ www.boss-publishing.com
Cover Designed by Emmanuel Johnson of B.O.S.S. Publishing

All rights reserved. Under International Copyright Law, no part of this publication may be reproduced, stored, or transmitted by any means- electronic, mechanical, photographic (photocopy), recorded, or otherwise-without written permission. For information address Joyce Reed, PO Box 669574, Marietta Ga. 30066

For information regarding special discounts for bulk purchases, sales promotions, speaking engagements and or book clubs. For details, please contact Joyce Reed at stolen1innocence@gmail.com or visit www.iamurvoice.com

Manufactured in the United States of America

ISBN-13: 978-1484987834
ISBN-10: 1484987837

Some letters in the story are the actual letters written word from word at a younger age.

If you are the copyright holders of these poems, or passages titled "unknown Authors" listed in this story, please contact me at www.iamurvoice.com and I will be happy to remove it if requested. Copied poems from www.scrapbook.com

10 9 8 7 6 5 4 3 2

CONTENTS

ACKNOWLEDGEMENTS
PREFACE
A Letter from the Author
GROWING UP ON MAY STREET   10
DEATH RISES   30
LOSING PART OF ME   46
THE STRUGGLE   62
MOTHERHOOD AT 15   88
DON'T JUDGE ME!!   108
MEN – VS – WOMEN   118
LOVES ALL – TRUST FEW!!!   132
FRIENDS & HATERS   140
LIES & BETRAYAL   148
MY OTHER LIFE   154
MY CHANGE, MY OUTCOME   178

ACKNOWLEDGEMENTS

I want to first and foremost thank GOD for allowing me to go through what I went through and make it out alive to be able to write this book, to help others that has been through what I've been through. If I didn't understand then, I understand now. I give much thanks to my children that has been a blessing to my life, since day one. Everyone that has believed in me since the beginning and never judged me, will always hold a special place in my heart. I thank the people that GOD has brought in my life to help make me the woman I am today and make Hurt Used To Live Here possible. Thanks to my Mentor Sandy, my editors Alicia and Dennis, my website designer Crystal and book cover designer Howard and Emmanuel and a host of friends and family. You always believed in me and never let me give up, even when I wanted to. Thank You all for everything, if it was for your love and support I don't think i would have gotten this far.

www.iamURvoice.com

Email: stolen1innicence@gmail.com

PREFACE

What you are about to read are stories about my life and events that took place between the ages of 9-23 years of age. The different subtitles represent different stories. This story you are about to read is true and told to you as I remember it. Some names have been changed to protect the innocent, the guilty, and the nasty. Take a ride with me back in time to find out what a innocent little girl was forced to deal with, starting at 9 years old. Feel free to put your seat belt on because it will be a bumpy ride. I share with you my life, how I lived it, and how I overcame it all. Today, I stand before you a great Mother, Author, entrepreneur and Leader. I'm here to take you to a place you never could imagine going or being. Never Judge a book by its cover, first open it and read it.

My name is Joyce and this is MY STORY!!

A Letter from the Author

Using the words I recorded in journals and notebooks I kept as a young girl, I now bare my soul within these pages by sharing my truth. I share my personal struggles with the world to help others and give them the support and love I never felt as a young girl. I don't want anyone to ever feel, what I felt growing up, but in my years of healing I realize that I am certainly not the only one. It was a lot of hurt and pain, but there are ways to get through it, to do more than just survive. Reclaim your worth, your dignity, your SELF. He will see you through it, and He will put people in your path that will help along the way.

I am sharing my story with you, so others, who have judged me without knowing the silent pain that I carried, will finally understand. "Never judge a book by its cover, first open it and read it." So as the Bible says, I am making it plain, and writing it on tablets--making my life that open book; a book that includes a vision of hope, faith and victory that many desire, but few have claimed.

At the end of my story, you will have cried, laughed, had chills or even gotten upset, felt hurt or felt love, but at the very end of it all I want you to take my words, and then write your own story, or rewrite your story with a new path of healing, love, and faith. Then you too can share with the world and change someone's life. It starts with a thought or the spoken word and ends with change. In the beginning was the word. And the two most powerful words on the planet are: I am. Anything behind that should be positive. So I will say that I am single mom of two wonderful boys, I am a business owner, I am a writer, I am a college graduate, I am a friend, I am a WOMAN, I am stubborn, I am real, I am a best friend, I am loving, I am worthy, I am forgiving, I am A fighter, I am a beautiful, "I AM" wonderful, I am GOD's child I am Joyce Reed and this is my journey.

Joyce Reed

ONE

Chapter 1

GROWING UP ON MAY STREET

It is said in my hometown of Chicago that Chicago can either make you or break you – in my case it actually did both. Surviving those mean streets has been a testament to my survival skills and the Grace of God.

The start of what I remember – I was born on January 17, 1982, around 9:30PM. My brother Michael and I are exactly 1 year and 4 days apart. I have a sister that has a different father but same mother as Michael and I. She is 3 years older than I am. That doesn't count all the other children my "my sperm donor" (father) has. I have 11 sisters and 1 other brother (that later was revealed to the family when he was around 15 years old) my sperm donor's youngest child is the same age as my youngest son. They are actually months apart. Papa was a rolling stone!

When I was around 4 or 5 my mother and father were married and I remember when my father used to hit and fight my mother. I remember one fight clear as day. My mom and dad were fighting downstairs in the living room, and me and my siblings were hiding in the corner by the closet. We were on the floor cuddled up as we cried and held each other in fear. All I can remember was my dad was chasing my mom around the house threatening to hurt her and she ran and ran until he eventually caught up to her and beat her continuously. Me my brother and my sister all ran in a

Joyce Reed

corner and held each other and screamed until it was over. I can't remember how it really ended because I was so young. I think was like 5 years old when this happened. Thankfully my mom ended up leaving him after that.

My mom got a divorce and ended up meeting this man named Billy years later after her and my dad got a divorce and we didn't like him because he used to wait until my mother would go to work and try to discipline us. He would whip us for no reason and make up lies to my mom as to why he had to whip us that day. I remember having to sit on the couch downstairs in the living room for hours and hours holding hands with my brother and sister. We were not allowed to do anything while my mother was gone. Billy just made us sit on the couch until it was time to go to bed. If we argued or fought, it was his cue to beat us. It was like he couldn't wait until we did something to whoop us. He sometimes did it just because or when he was angry with my mom. I was tired of getting beat for no reason and no one would ever listen to us. So one day, I packed my things and left the house. I was so little; I had to be around 6 or 7 years old. I knew my cousin stayed close so I tried walk to her house which was right across the alley. I didn't even make it up the back stairs before he was right there and he whipped me continuously until my mother came home from work. He left whips and marks all over my body. My mother always worked and we rarely got to see her, so when I finally got the chance to show her my marks they had already disappeared.

My mom worked 3 jobs sometimes to support us but at that time I just thought she didn't love us and wanted to be away from us. When it was time to be loved I knew fun, money, clothes would be involved. We had anything we wanted, all the name brand clothes and shoes, hair done every 2 weeks, and got allowance weekly (only if we did our chores.) My mom was a clean freak so everything had to be perfect. My mom cleaned with pure bleach every night. It would make us sneeze and cough due to the strong fumes. It would be so bad that sometimes we would go to school still smelling bleach. She didn't seem to care. She just had to have a perfectly clean house. She was very organized and neat. If you needed anything, my mom knew where to find it and it was definitely labeled. She even kept file cabinets for each of her kids. My mom kept receipts until the ink was gone .She was out of control. My mom was so neat that when we would go to a restaurant she would clean the table off for them, or if we would go to a hotel she would make her own bed up. It wasn't because she didn't want them in the room she just had to clean and that was her thing. Some people like to drink or smoke, or work on cars, or even steal but my mom's thing was cleaning and organizing. Even when she would wash clothes she was so tedious with it – she washed all white, all pinks, all yellows, all blacks, all socks, etc… Yes! It was that bad, some of the things rubbed off on me but not all. LOL

My "sperm donor" (father) was a business owner and that's what I learned from him. Not to ever work for anyone! I'm glad that is the only thing I did learn from him being your own boss.
He was a business owner but he was mean and treated people like they were shit and beneath him. Karma hit his ass real quick. He ended up getting beat up by 10 guys with bats and bricks, which left him in a body cast. It didn't stop him from being the asshole he had always been. Even though he was not in our lives like he should have been, he made sure he was available when it was time for us to get a beating. I can't say a whipping because that would be an understatement. When my "sperm donor" beat me,

he would make my skin bleed.

Is that normal?

Is someone going to say something to him?

I could feel my skin burning as I got in the shower. Eventually the marks would heal and leave dark colored marks on my body but I knew I would get beat more if I told someone.

Side Job:

To keep active and out of trouble my brother and I came up with a great idea. On the side we would make extra money by smashing cans. My mom eventually supported the idea and got us a can smasher that was nailed to the wall in the kitchen in the basement where we lived on May Street. We made an extra $5.00 a piece and we split that a week and we used to split that between us. We headed straight to the candy store and ate it all up – a hundred and fifty pieces a piece and used the other dollar for some chips and juice to wash it all down. That's when candy was a penny. I suffered later in life with cavities but at that time what child cares about cavities or worrying about eating too much candy?

Love vs. Money:

I used to feel that my mom would sometimes buy our love. When we needed advice or someone to talk to my mom was not the communicator at all. I still have letters that I wrote my mom to talk to her about and relay messages. I learned at a young age that writing was the best way to communicate to her and others. We didn't want for anything and we went places and had a great time. That was all fun but what a child needs is love. They need to be held, hugged, and given confirmation that everything will be ok. They want to hear, I am here for you, I love you and will protect you. Did I blame my mother, yes, I did. Do I understand now? Yes, I do. So telling my mom about her boyfriend Billy was something that I could not do because she worked too much and needed the help after her divorce. I only understand now why she wasn't there, but I'm still trying to put my finger on why she didn't listen to us and protect us. After a year my mother finally left Billy. I guess it was because we would complain and run away a lot. We were happy about that. We finally had our mom to ourselves but we were wrong. She was still the same working mom. She was a single mom, so she had to do what she had to do to make ends meet.

The start of something different:

When I turned 7 she met a man by the name of Bug and he had three kids of his own and we were a happy family again. We now had a stepbrother and two stepsisters, and they were our age. We went everywhere together and had fun. Even the small things made us happy -like going to the park or having picnics and BBQs at the park. He was nice to us and it was a plus that he had children that were in our age group. It made it a lot easier to adjust. Me and all the girls would get together in our basement and make up dance routines and practice them for a week and get the parents together and show them what we had been working on. I was always the shy one in the group with no rhythm at all. I danced like a white girl, as they say. It was like my body was stuck to the ground and frozen and I was dancing to my own beat. Everyone would be mad at me because I just couldn't get the dance routine together for anything in the world. They sometimes just left me out of it. We had family night on Fridays. We would all get together and

Joyce Reed

play board games, spades, and Nintendo games and atari all night until we all passed out in the living room on the floor. We never really got in trouble and in the beginning there was no fighting between my mom and him at all. I just thought my life was perfect and I had everything I ever wanted. My step brother and sisters eventually moved in with us on May Street. Before they moved in, it would be so sad to see them have to go home to their mom's house in Iowa. We knew it would be a long time before we would see them again. We all begged for them to move in with us. When it was time for Bug to take them home, we would cry until next time. Someone got tired of it, so if anything needed to be done and fixed then Michael was the go to person. If you needed your tires flattened or your windows busted, or even a distraction for a while he was definitely the go to boy. My brother once told them that he would flatten Bug's tires so they could never go back home. That was the day that they moved with us. They couldn't miss any more days of school, so they just transferred to Chicago schools. It was perfect for all of us.

We found room in the 6 bedroom house on May Street. All the fun lasted a few years.

The Tables Turn:

My mother was a happy person then. She never really whipped us at all anyway. She just allowed her partners to do it. It went from a few hits to get in the tub and don't dry off, now go hold the pole in the living room and get beat with the extension cord over and over again. We had belt marks and whips all over our bodies. After getting beat like that, it would only make me want to do more damage and be even worse. My brother and I would do crazy things like: break things and lie about it, get each other in trouble, or he would stick marbles in his nose so he wouldn't have to go to school. I would do other things like go to school and announce that I had ringworm in a place that couldn't be seen while my catholic uniform was on. I just didn't like school so I did what I could to be out. I was only in 4th grade and hated school then. Maybe I didn't like school because I was transferred 5 times but went to 4 different schools. If I could go back and be a kid again I would have never missed a day of school and did extra work. No matter what I always had good grades in school. Even though I hated it, it was fun once you were there. The part I hated was going to bed early or waking up at the crack of dawn .We went to a Catholic school so we had to be there at 7AM in the morning and we had to catch the bus because my mom had to work of course. Mass would be on Tuesday and Thursday. We would have to pray to Mary. I didn't like that either because at home my mom was a Jehovah's Witness along with my granny and grandma they were true believers. I was so confused but didn't complain because I didn't listen to any of it anyway. I was young and didn't really care, I was ready to get into more trouble, well not trouble but be a kid and have fun in the sun and enjoy life. I was in a Catholic school going to Mass and on Wednesday and Sunday I would study to be a Jehovah's Witness.

Was I really supposed to understand any of it? I was confused the whole time! It's like you trying to teach a baby how to speak Spanish at home but only speak English around him. He would eventually learn English before Spanish. Later on in the process he was confused because he was hearing one thing but instilled to learn what they wanted him to learn. At school I learned to pray for Mary and at home I learned that Heaven was colorful and you couldn't do certain things like celebrating holidays. We only celebrated birthdays and it seem like we had Bible study every other day.

Park Disaster:

One day one of my step sisters and I were sneaking out to go to the park because we were on punishment and we decided to go on our own and I paid for it. It was around 9 in the morning. We both walked to the park that was just right down the street from May Street, more like 3 blocks away from the house and back then it was ok for two young girls to walk to the park and not have to look around to see if someone was trying to rob or snatch you. The world is not like it used to be at all. I remember being able to play outside, walk to the store, and get on the bus without a beating, or robbery, or even a killing taking place. It used to be ok. As we got to the park with no worries, all we could see were opportunities to play and have fun while Bug was still cooking breakfast back at home on May Street. There was this thing that we used to do – see how high you can swing and then jump off while you are still swinging.
Ok! I can do this!
"I thought to myself."

I've seen this done so many times and I knew I could do it because I wasn't your typical girly girl. I was a little tom boy. So I was confident in the decision I made. While we were on the swing, we swung really high and my stepsisters jumped off first landing safely on the ground. Then it was my turn. I wanted to swing higher and try to jump off to show off and prove to her that I could go higher than she did but I did the opposite. I flew

Hurt Used To Live Here

off going backwards and when I flipped over I landed on my face and I hit my face on some bricks. My sister was screaming and crying and yelling because I was not moving or responding at all. I thought I was alert and knew what was going on around me and I could hear everything that was going on but my body wouldn't move at all. My sister tried to pick me up and walk me home but I passed out in the middle of the street and that's really all that I remember. I found out later that I was in and out of consciousness .My sister said she was screaming for help and trying to hold me up at the same time. There were two girls walking our way and my sister asked them as she was screaming and yelling, to help her. She was screaming, "Someone please help me. My sister, my sister! "Can you please hold my sister while I get help? "She asked as my face was bleeding profusely. The two girls grabbed each arm and carried me out of the street. She told them that we stayed two blocks away. The two girls held me up while my sister ran home for help. When I woke up and came to, I was in the hospital getting CT scans and everyone was there. I was told that my face was full of blood and my mom thought that my teeth were missing and I would need stitches in my face. Thank GOD that was not the case at all. I was allowed to go home the same day but my mom had to monitor me and wake me up every two hours for 24 hours just in case I went to sleep and ended up unconscious from blunt force head trauma. It was really bad. All the blood I saw in my granny's car on the ride home was crazy. The backseat was full of blood and she had blue seats in her Grand Marquis. I thought my teeth were gone too but thank GOD I was fine.

    The day after that incident I was back outside playing with my brother and the other kids. It didn't faze me at all. At this point of my life, I had already broken my ring finger by playing toss

Joyce Reed

outside in the front of the house. My brother and I were throwing the softball back and forth to each other when he decided that I was a pro basketball player and threw the ball so hard that it bent my finger all the way back and made my finger touch the top of my hand. Mind you, I was not flexible at all. I didn't want to go to the doctor, so I wrapped it with a metal board and taped it and went back to playing. A little broken finger wasn't going to stop me.

Life Changing:

When I was 12, my brother and I, our next door neighbor, and my friend Renee that lived across the alley from me decided to walk to the park. While we were crossing the street, me and my next door neighbor were holding hands, My brother and Renee were holding hands just a few feet away from us. We called ourselves liking each other, you know kid stuff. We were crossing the street to get to the park and there was this nice guy who stopped for us to let us get across the street. We didn't cross at the stop sign because it was easier to cross in the middle of the street. It would take if you cut you right in front of the park. It was a huge van that let us go by, as me and my next door neighbor walked first in front of the van a woman came from nowhere going almost 60 MPH and ran the stop sign. She hit us! All I heard was a bomb and screech with glass smashing. My next door neighbor tried to push me out of the way to prevent me from getting hit head on because I was on the side where the car was coming from, but I still hit my head on the windshield, then I flew across the street from the impact and landed right in front of the park. He went through the windshield. I just cracked it and bounced back off. I tried to get up because it just felt like I bumped my head and was a little shook up, but when I tried to stand up I couldn't. I fell right back down. My right leg was bent all the way backward. When I saw that, I passed out because my leg was bent in a backwards U position. I heard a girl yell "you better act like you dead" and then I fainted, not because she told me to but after seeing my leg bent backwards it made me pass right back out. It was like something you see on TV or what I used to do with all my Barbie dolls when I didn't want them anymore. It felt like my legs were missing. I had no feeling in them at all. The lady that hit us stopped the car and came to offer me a pillow. I really didn't know what was going on at that point as I was in and out. I didn't know where my next door neighbor was or my friend Renee or if my brother was even gone. All I heard was different voices and when I did come to, there were a lot of people surrounding me. I then heard the ambulance coming and my mother's voice saying "Does she have on her school shoes?" I would never forget that, not is my baby ok or anything she was worried about my shoes more than me. We were not allowed to wear our school shoes outside, at all. When we first got home we had to change our school clothes and put on our play clothes before we went outside. My mom was so strict on that too. As they put me in the ambulance and closed the door and we prepared to pull off – my bed was not connected to the bars and the bed hit the back door and at that point I thought I was dead. Not literally, because it was kind of funny. I saw this in a movie so I was laughing in my head because I couldn't verbally say anything, I'm like what's next!?!?!

    I arrived at the hospital on a body board and a neck brace in a lot of pain. They took x-rays of my body and a CT scan again of my head. The results were that the driver had chipped a piece of

Joyce Reed

my patella and the doctors said that eventually that little piece would break off. I never paid it any mind because I was only 12 and my knee was the last thing that I was worried about. I was young and ready to get back outside and I did in a couple of days. My next door neighbor was ok too. He had over 30 stitches in his ear and he had a few bruises and bumps but we were alive. All my hair fell out due to all the glass that was in my hair. I had to wear ugly braids to make my hair grow back. 10 years later a piece of my patella eventually fell off and now you can literally feel it moving under my knee cap. I had to get pins and screws in my knee to hold it in place and was on crutches for 6 months and those were the worst 6 months ever. Being dependent on someone is the worst feeling ever. I hated not being mobile. Due to the surgery, I developed arthritis in my right knee and now it hurts worse than before I even got my surgery, there would be times that I would just be walking and my knee would just go out on me. I would feel like I only had one leg. I would also fall down flights of stairs or trip over something really small. Then there were times that I was not able to walk for long periods of time because of the aching. Even now if I drive for a long period of time it feels like my bones are grinding and rubbing together every inch I make. Driving in traffic is very painful at times too when it's a lot of stop and go.

If I wanted I could be a meteorologist because I know when it's going to rain or snow outside, because of the feeling I get in my knee. It causes my knee to ache so bad that I could barely walk or sleep at night. It has been said on web md that: "When pressure in the environment changes, we know that the amount of fluid in the joint or the pressure inside the joint fluctuates with it," "Individuals with arthritic joints feel these changes much more because they have less cartilage to provide cushioning." I don't think I have any cushion at all!

I remember the lady that hit us came to the house with flowers for me after I got out of the hospital and my brother answered the basement door, took the flowers from the lady and smacked her with them. He then told her that she better not ever come back again and no one wanted her flowers. He then slammed the door in her face. That's just how Michael was. He was very over protective of me – anyone that messed with me; he would make sure he was known as the big brother. Later, we were told that we were jaywalking and it was illegal. WOW! As far as money, from the accident I don't know what happened to it or if I even got paid. The only person that will know is my mother. She told me later on that she paid for my medical bills but we were on public assistance.

Being a kid:

Yeah, we went to Moo and Oink with a book of stamps and a list for our mom. We hated walking home with all those bags in the cart, but liked to actually shop in the store to find things. I used to like going down the bread and cupcake aisle and smash the bread and the cupcakes with my fingers. I was a kid that had to touch everything that looked interesting to me. I wanted to know how everything felt. I eventually stopped when I heard on the news years later that a guy got caught in Dominick's smashing bread and was arrested. I got scared and stopped immediately!

Joyce Reed

Creepy House:

I have experienced a lot in my younger days. I heard ghost stories and real life stories that my family has seen, heard, or experienced while living on May Street. I was told that someone brought a Ouija board in the house and after it was tampered with there were some scary things going on like: talking dolls and toy robots coming to life only at night, lights flickering on and off, doors slamming, sprits walking past you, voices and anything else scary you can imagine. I can recall when I was a little girl, I remember this vaguely, there was a toy robot that my brother used to play with all the time and he would sometimes get up in the middle of the night and go sit in the closet with the robot and every time he would be found, he would be in a daze like his mind was still sleep but his body was there. He was like in a zombie state; we would ask how did he get there? Still to this day I don't know what was going on; on May Street. Did the Ouija board bring bad demons or bad spirits in the house? Was the house cursed or haunted? I would tell my friends about the things that I experienced and they would just laugh at me and think I was crazy. So many things happened on May Street that if I talk about them all then it would be a book in itself. At the end of it all they had to bring a priest in to get rid of whatever has entered or whomever they let in from playing with that Ouija board. It was even impossible to get rid of it because after throwing it in the dumpster in the alley, it magically appeared back in the closet. That's when a priest came in. Everyone doesn't believe in ghosts, or spirits or even demons but until you have experienced seeing, hearing, and feeling them then I wouldn't believe it either. Not only have I experienced these things too while several people have seen what we have been trying to tell people, such as lights getting dim then bright, door knobs twisting with no one in the other room on the other side of the door, doors being slammed closed, shadows walking, feeling a very cold presence, and hearing voices. The scariest moment were sitting in my bed and seeing it sink in like someone was sitting down next to me and I knew I was the only one there. There were even times that I would wake up to a sprit standing over me. Still no one was there to say baby, let me put my arm around you and comfort you. Instead we got the twisted face like "yeah right" or "whatever girl, go sit down." I just had to act like nothing was happening and keep it moving. Was this normal, because it was far from normal to me?

Being the Youngest:

I guess since I was the baby, I endured so much abuse from my siblings; like black eyes, spritz sprayed in my eyes, hair being pulled, and being told what to do. I had to clean up behind them, get in trouble for them, and even get punched in the chest because my brother was so curious to find out what was growing under my shirts. He was too young to understand but didn't care to find out, even after telling him that punching me there would stop the growth. He didn't stop. I decided to return the favor and start kicking him in the balls when he punched me in my chest as hard as he could. He would then find out that it wasn't a good feeling after all. I would go ouch and he would go ugh. I think that's a feeling, a woman would never feel but I think we feel something very close to it or maybe worse than getting kicked in the balls. Like, when a woman rides a bike ladies and falls on the pole of the bike. If you have ever done that before, just saying it brings that pain back shooting through your body. Ouchhhh!!

Joyce Reed

Memory Lane:

There is another story I want to share about what went on May Street. Our house was the "go to" house for everything. We had sisters and brothers and were always playing ball in the alley, playing rope with the girls in the front, playing hop scotch, rock paper scissors, find a girl kiss a boy, and all of the hand games. We would even played Teacher. No matter what, we found something to do and as long as we were in front of the house when the street lights came on we were ok to stay out longer. We got smart and decided to cut the wires on the boxes to the poles on the block and when it was time to come in front of the house when the streets lights came on, our excuse was they didn't come on. If we had rules, we always found ways to go around them or get out of it.

There was an incident that happened with a group of friends on May Street, We were into it with a girl that was messing with one of my sister's boyfriends and we all stuck together even if we knew they were wrong. One day some people decided to break in the girl's house and give her house a new makeover by throwing black, green, and yellow paint on all her house and on her things. They poured paint all on her couches, beds, carpet, kitchen, fans, clothes, and on everything that was not pinned down. My cousin and I were told to go look for our sisters and brothers and we did just that. When we got there we saw some of them jumping out of windows and running out of back doors screaming grab this and run. We had food, pillows, and clothes thrown at us and were told to go hide them at home. Later that day the police came to our house and questioned everyone about the break-in and all I knew was that I had nothing to do with it; but I wasn't about to tell either. I told the police that I didn't see or hear about anything.

As the police was questioning all of us, he felt that something wasn't right. The police flashed the light on my sister's shoes and found the same paint from the house on her shoes. We all got put punishment for the break-in, and I got in trouble for being an accessory to the crime. Everyone was pissed at my sister and made sure she knew it too. We had to go back to her house and scrub the paint off of everything that was there. Thankfully, her mom didn't press charges against us. That was the worst day ever, due to me not even being there but I got myself involved when I took the items to hide them. I was an accessory to the crime.

Fireworks to remember:

There was a time when all bad things started to happen in our neighborhood. It was mostly just gang retaliations. One day we had just left Rainbow Beach on 79th. We ended our night with fireworks in Racine Park, the same park where I busted my face. As we are watching the fireworks and playing we heard 3 gun shots and we all fell to the ground. After the shooting had stopped we all gathered together in a huddle and walked home together. As we got to our block on 76 th street we saw a boy lying down by a building in the alley he was lying face up with blood rushing out of his head and his body was jumping and bouncing all over the place but he wasn't saying a word. He was just squirming. After about two minutes his body stopped all movements. He just laid there lifeless. His brains were all on the basement window of someone's apartment by the alley. That was the first time that I have ever seen a dead body and especially done execution style. We were all scared to go to sleep that night but realized that this was just the beginning of all the violence that would happen on May Street. I have witnessed several shootings. A lady was found dead in our alley and her body was pushed in a trash can bent in a backwards U.

I also experienced seeing gang beatings, drive by's, stick ups, and anything else that you can imagine that happened on and around the Auburn Gresham area.

By experiencing all of these things in life, it made me more aware of my surroundings, and I became streets smart. It's great to be book smart but being raised in the hood; to survive you need to also be street smart as well. These streets will eat you up and spit you out if you are not careful.

There is nothing like a Smart dumb ass!!!

A bit of advice: Never walk the same way home as you do going. Always switch your route up. You have to know who is behind you without even turning your body to look. You need to know who your friends are and always stay ahead of everyone. LOVE ALL, TRUST FEW!

Hurt Used To Live Here

Joyce Reed

TWO

Chapter 2

DEATH RISES

October 3, 1991, at around 6:00AM in the morning, I found out what losing someone close felt like. I was getting ready for Catholic school and was forced to put on an ugly burgundy and plaid outfit with a white butterfly collar uniform. I can't forget the long burgundy socks we had to wear with the black Mary Janes. I hated that uniform! Anyway, as I was putting my uniform on, I heard a loud bang over my head! My mom ran upstairs – I was scared so I ran too.

Bang, bang, bang, my uncle and mom are banging on the bathroom door – no one replied so my uncle was forced to break down the door. The door came open and I saw my great grandma on the floor. She had slipped out of the tub and hit her head on the radiator. I saw her for only about three seconds then they closed the door and as I listened at the door I heard my granny say: "I love you all and make sure you tell those kids to stay in school and be good." At that moment I knew what losing a loved one felt like at 9-years old. You were told that they go to Heaven but I didn't understand why. I was just getting to know my granny. My granny was laid to rest at the age of 84. I was sad and emotional but I don't really remember anything after the funeral. I do remember she used to make me the best rice pudding in the world. She always made me my own bowl and no one was to touch it. That's what I do remember about my granny. She was caring, loving, beautiful, and loved to cook. I recall when I went to her room one night to tell her I loved her and as I walked in her room with no shoes or socks on (my mom hated when we walked around with no shoes on she said it will make our feet big or cold would set up in our feet from the cold floor) by not listening I got a half an inch from her bed and stepped on an old rusted nail and it went into my entire foot. My granny used her old remedies and made it feel all better.

I learned that if you are not as close to your family you need to put all the drama, excuses, hurt, pain, rebellion and pettiness to the side and get to know your family. Life is too short to hold a grudge. I was actually too young to have a long relationship with my granny because God called her home when I was a baby myself. Some of you have great grandmothers that are still alive to this day and cherish those moments and get to know your family history and learn what the world was like without reading it on TV. Learn what the truth is – love until you can't love anymore.

Lost in the World so Young:

When I was around 11 or 12 my aunt had a best friend by the name of Deyon, and they always used to hang out together a lot. Deyon had a daughter and her name was also Deyon. We called them Lil Deyon and Big Deyon. We were the same age, just like 2 weeks apart and we started going to the same elementary school and walking home together. Lil Deyon's auntie stayed about 3 blocks from the school we attended and since I wasn't in that school district I was using someone else's address. Some days walking home with Deyon after school was cool until my mom or auntie came to pick me up. That's where all my friends were anyway so I loved it over there. I hated going home, because it was boring and I had no one to play with. We became so close that my mom ended up adopting her and taking full custody of Lil Deyon. Her mom was not the worst but wasn't the best either and didn't want to change her ways anytime soon. My mom took on the responsibility of caring for this misguided little girl. My mom actually would take anyone in that needed help. She was a good hearted person. I was excited because I had someone my own age to play with. My other brothers and sisters from my step dad had to go back and live with their mom in Milwaukee after a while so I was lonely again – so this was perfect for me. We talked about a lot, had sleepovers, and shared so many secrets. One secret that she did share with me when she was 10-years old was that she never wanted to go back home with her mom, ever again. One day Lil Deyon overheard a conversation that Big Deyon was going to try to get her back and once Lil Deyon heard that, she was scared and didn't want to go back, so Lil Deyon came up with this plan to get on her bike and ride until she thought her mom came and left. We both laughed at the idea and said deal! I told her that I would come to the alley and look for her in about an hour or so and give her the clear that her mom came and left. We hugged each other and said I love you and see you later. Not knowing that that would be the last time I would see her face alive. Lil Deyon was not an average body built girl. She was built like she was a 21year old woman but had a baby face. You knew she was a little girl up close but from a distance you would think she was a woman by her curves and full figure. She was a troubled girl due to her upbringing, which was not her fault. She had a rough life but was very sweet and I understood her. Lil Deyon ended up meeting this guy on the way to get away from her mom. Lil Deyon got tired of riding the bike so she started to walk the bike. A man saw her walking by and tried to talk to her and somehow he talked her into coming into his house. There was a gun on the table and Lil Deyon went to grab it and he took it away from her.

He then began to show her the gun and Bang! It went off and shot her in her chest. I was at home waiting patiently for her to pull up in the alley and there was no Lil Deyon. After a while my mom called the police and of course you could not file a missing person report until after being missing for twenty-four hours. They just thought that she was just a runaway.

My mom got a call after days and days of waiting from someone asking her to come identify a body that was brought matching the description of your missing person. She was told that it was brought in days ago with no identification. I can only imagine what my mom was feeling hearing those words. My mom ended up going to identify the body and calling her biological mom Big Deyon to come along. My mom walked in and as they unzipped the body bag and there was Lil Deyon lying there dark and lifeless. She was sitting there for days and no one even knew or said anything, but that would be too much like right for the police to do their real jobs. My heart was hurt so badly because this is where I'm like REALLY two deaths of my loved ones. Why? Is GOD real and why did he let this happen again I asked? She was a child, a baby; she didn't even live her life. It just started and ended just like that. I always had questions with little or no answers. Lil Deyon was laid to rest on 8/5/1994. I lost my great grandma and now my sister.

Tom Boy:

By mommy working all the time – 3 jobs at a time and we were always together and spending our time together – I used to play basketball and football with him and the boys. I would rather hang with boys because girls were about boys and kissing and sleeping with them. I was more like a tom boy when I was younger. I didn't like girly things that much but my cabbage patch doll and my kid sister doll (that's because my brother had the kid brother doll). All my dolls had to have a bald head, because I didn't like the long pretty hair. I liked dangerous things like putting my tongue on a cold pole, playing ding dong ditch, and playing sports. We would also run from people after me and my brother threw something at them. We were both daring and dangerous together. We had so much fun together. If you saw Michael you saw me. We were connected by hip. If he wanted to go somewhere and he got in trouble I would take the blame and vice versa.

Dropping like Flies:

A few weeks later my grandmother on my mother's side had a stroke at home. She was getting ready for the doctor and she fell and hit her head on the night stand. She cut her feet at the same time while trying to get ready and had blood everywhere. I was in the kitchen and she was walking around the house like everything was ok. I yelled when I saw her face and said sit down you are bleeding everywhere. She went on to say that she was ok and it was a little cut. "Leave me alone so I can get ready for the doctor," she yelled. This was the 3rd or 4th stroke my grandmother had within a few months. It was devastating to have to see her going through that.

Joyce Reed

I spent my days after school teaching my grandmother how to read, write, and spell over again. Sometimes it got frustrating because I would miss hanging out with friends. Months went by and granny learned more than just words she learned how to curse again and cursed like a sailor. She would always curse my best friend Nicole out and tell her that she needs to go home and stay out of her kitchen. She sometimes chased us with her broom around the house. She couldn't control what really came out of her mouth due to the strokes she had. She would say one thing but meant something else. My grandmother was not the person to use curse words at all. It just changed her in so many ways but I was just glad that she was here.

Until one day in October of 1996 my granny was rushed to the ER due to her 4th stroke and they kept her this time because the cuts on her feet were not healing right. My granny was a diabetic and the cut on her foot caused an infection called gangrene and within 2 hours it had traveled halfway up her leg. The hospital called the family and told the family to come down immediately as the infection was spreading. The family got there and they informed us that they had to do emergency surgery to amputate her leg in order to stop the infection from spreading more. The family decided to go ahead. Before they got prepped for surgery the gangrene had spread to the entire left side of her body and she passed away within 20 minutes of them getting her prepared for surgery. This was the 4th death in our family in 5 months.

WHY GOD???

WHY ME???

Hurt Used To Live Here

My Granny Glo was one of a kind:

My grandma Glo's husband, which was my grandfather also on my mom's side, passed away on 08/07/1996 from a dog bite that turned into an infection. His alcohol addiction caused the infection not to heal properly and it killed him slowly. It was kind of crazy because I couldn't attend my grandmother's funeral on my "sperm donor" side of the family because it was the same day as my grandfather's funeral. I was attending funerals like kids go to the candy store. I had to wear my same black dress for my aunt and my granny's funeral. My great auntie Bernice died 24 days later on 8/31/1996 from cancer. Her sister and sister's husband died 24 days apart and she lost her battle to cancer 2 months later. "I don't think you guys heard me," I lost my grandfather, my grandmother on my sperm donor side (she also lost her battle to lupus the same month my grandfather passed away.) My great aunt, my cousin got killed (he was shot over 20 times by a rival gang in September of 1996,) and then my grandma on my mom's side. I lost 6 people in 1996 –so far my number is 8 people passing away in my family. I had to ask, is this really happening to me? I should be going crazy!

Enough is enough:

I tried to attempt suicide by taking 35 pills and that didn't work, it backfired on me. It actually caused me to throw up a huge pile of vomit. Throwing up my insides, I couldn't eat for 3 days due to a sore stomach. I never tried that again. What else was I supposed to do at this point? I felt that GOD wasn't real; he let me down time after time. I felt numb and dead anyway. After all of this happened to me, I felt that GOD was not my biggest supporter.

I thought he was punishing me for something and I had no idea what I had done. I was a kid that couldn't take anymore. I used to think that I was the devil's child because everything seemed to happen in 6's ... 6's deaths in 96. I had one more time that something happened in 6's and I would have been convinced that I was the devil's child.....

In Loving Memory Of

Deyon Renee Parker

August 23, 1994

Visitation: 1:00 PM   Service: 1:30 PM

Gatling's Chapel
10133 South Halsted Street
Chicago, Illinois 60628

Rev. Henry - Officiating

In Loving Memory Of

Ruth Whitney

SUNDAY, OCTOBER 6, 1991

Wake – 7:00 P.M.   Funeral – 7:30 P.M.

KINGDOM HALL
1432 West 79th Street
Chicago, Illinois

Brother William Pace, Sr. – Officiating

In Loving Memory of

1936 — 1996

Gloria Whitney-Collins

Obituary

Order of Service

Tributes

In Memory of

Bernice Whitney Turner

January 18, 1925 ~ August 31, 1996

Services:
Friday ~ September 6, 1996
Wake - 10:00 A.M. - Funeral - 10:30 A.M.

Leak & Sons Funeral Chapels

7838 South Cottage Grove Avenue
Chicago, Illinois

In Loving Memory Of

Mr. Raymond Sloan, Sr.

Thursday, March 19, 1998

Visitation: 11:30 - 12:00 P.M.   Service: 12:00 - 1:00 P.M.

Gatling's Chapel

10133 South Halsted Street
Chicago, Illinois 60628

Reverend Donald J. Ehr
Officiating

In Loving Memory Of
Raymond Sloan, Jr.
1954 ~ 2000

WEDNESDAY, AUGUST 23, 2000

Visitation: 11:30 ~ 12:00 P.M.   Service: 12:00 ~ 1:00 P.M.

GATLING'S CHAPEL
10133 South Halsted Street
Chicago, Illinois 60628

Rev. Dr. Benjamin Garrett, Officiating

Joyce Reed

THREE

Chapter 3

LOSING PART OF ME

When I needed YOU:

My father wasn't in my life like he should have been, but I guess he was just being a typical man. I was used to it all my life. My mother wasn't there either mentally or emotionally. I wanted to hear that everything was going to be ok, or come here baby; give me a hug, or even I LOVE YOU!!! I would have given up everything I had that was material to get the love I was missing.

Advice: Money can't buy you love and if you think buying love is real love, then you need to re-evaluate yourself. It takes more than money and name brand clothes to raise a child.

The Change:

Now after Lil Deyon's death I was able to let go and forgive and move on with my life. My family really didn't grieve any about deaths or losses. I became the same way. Keep it moving – two years passed and my life was better again. I got closer with my brother and further away from my sister. She was the oldest of us three – so she didn't like us to bother her at all. My brother and I tried to just stay away from her. Michael and I had gotten so close that we tagged team up against her. We played jokes on her and made sure that her hate would be for a reason. We would take her things from her room which she really loved. We would use her phone and run up the bill, so my mom would think it was her doing it. We just did things to her that would really give her a reason not to like us.

I remember when my brother Michael wanted to grow his hair and I was left to put the puffy tiny pony tails in his head. The girls liked it too. He had me put puff balls in his hair and thought that was cute. I would sit there for hours parting his hair in little sections and putting rubber bands in it to make this little puff balls that he loved. We grew so close that after a while it didn't bother me to do it. I actually started enjoying myself.

He was light skin with brown eyes, he was short and skinny with clear skin that he made sure he maintained on a daily basis. He had the cutest freckles that he got from his sperm donor side. I was thankful that my face was covered with them. He had a crocked tooth in the front from my oldest sister when we were younger. We were all at the park, I can't recall because I was too little but my mom told the story and I can picture every little detail.

As my sis was swinging on the swing high my brother runs right in front of the swing that my sister is on and she kicks him right in the face and that's how my brother's front teeth became crocked.

He also had a stuttering problem that he suffered from for a while, he went to speech to help with it, and it stared to get better when he would take a deep breath before speaking but it didn't stop the girls from loving him. I would tease him a lot about it and he would tease me about a lot of things also so we were even. It was brother and sister love but we never harmed each other only when he would try to be over protective. On another note, my

Hurt Used To Live Here

brother and step dad, Bug, really never got along at all.

He was a tall, with fair skin and had the tiniest eyes and had burns all over his arms, from a fire that happened earlier in his child hood. He stood about 6 feet 2 inches but overall he was an ok guy to me. I was always told not to trust a man with little eyes, for some reason my theory was true. My mom met him after she and my father had divorced when I was around 4-years old and right after Billy, the mean man that beat us all the time. I was just happy that Billy was no longer there and it was much better when my mom was happy.

Even the small things made us happy like going to the park, picnics and BBQ's all the time. He was nice to us and it was a plus that he had children that were in our age group. It was 2 girls and a boy that was in our age group and we clicked like that.

It all went left when Bug got mixed up with the wrong crowd. He started doing drugs smoking crack and stealing from the family but my mother was blind to the fact that he was doing all this. Growing up around other crack heads and drug addicts, it wasn't hard to pick up on it real fast--that he was truly on drugs. I don't think a person that is not a crack head will hang around another crack heads. The likely hood of that is slim to none.

Bug started to beat my mother and she would walk around with black eyes and had to go to work like that. I really don't know what the arguments would be about but all I knew was that me and my brother would try to tune it out and cut the television up or play the radio really loud. I really felt bad for my mom because she was up against a man that was twice her size and all she could do was just take the punches and leaving was my option but that wasn't for me to decide.

My mother worked two jobs to support her family, so she

49

was never really home. My mother never really talked about her personal relationship to us and she never set us down to tell us that this is wrong and to never live your life like this. What my mom did do was allow us to endure such violence and abuse daily. As I grew up I thought that if a man hit you he loved you. If he yelled he cared. Was I given any reason to think otherwise? They fought and she stayed. Why? I asked! Why can't she leave this man that is abusing her and keeping her ugly? My mom did fight back but fighting against a 250 lbs. man is difficult when my mom was 5'0" and weighing around 135 lbs. It only had gotten worse, when one day a fight had broken out upstairs in my sister's room and Bug stood over my mother and beat her and beat her. Me and my brother had gotten tired of it at this point because we knew he was on drugs and he would only continue if he knew that no one was there to help her or beat his ass for hitting a woman. What me and my brother did was un forgettable. I first jumped on top of him as he is on top of my mother beating her in her face and I jumped on his back and he threw me off of him and I hit my back on the corner of my sister's dresser drawer. When my brother saw that he was trying to hurt me too he went to go get a knife and came back into the room and swung it at him and cut him on his arm .This is when Bug realize that we wasn't taking anymore and you were going to leave our mother alone. We both screamed and yelled "Leave my mommy alone, leave her alone you fuckin crack head." He eventually walked away and like anything else we dealt with we all went too slept and the next day was like any of it never happened.

Hurt Used To Live Here

LIFE CHANGING:

The afternoon of May 15, 1996, Michael told me that he was sick and didn't feel good. I knew immediately his sugar was low, because he was a diabetic. So I had to fix him something to eat to get his sugar up again, after he had taking his insulin. This was nothing out of the ordinary. I fixed him his favorite, which was bacon. After making him a few strips, I made sure he was cool and told him I was going down the street to my friend's house, and that if he wanted me that is where I would be. I went down the street to my friend's house and I ate some of her mom's favorite homemade cornbread made from scratch.

Um Um good! I knew at this point Michael was ok because he never came to my friend's house to say otherwise, so I went on with my day. This day didn't feel right to me at all but I continued with it like any other day. I had so much on my mind, I just didn't feel at least at all but just couldn't put my finger on it.

My brother and my step father had just gotten into an argument about something stupid a few nights before and I felt something was wrong but didn't know why I was feeling like this. I left my friend's house and I went back to check on him but a few hours had passed by then and it was like around 7:00pm, so I went in the house to look for him and he was nowhere to be found. It was unusual for him to just disappear, especially without telling me because we were so close and we told each other everything and if you saw him you would have also seen me. He was my best friend, brother, protector, listener, and body guard. It was getting later and later and still no signs of Michael – this was the same feeling I felt when Lil Deyon never returned. When I noticed that he had left his hair pick and his favorite blue red and white Indian's baseball cap I told my stepfather that he was not in the house and that he never leaves his hat. He said, "He will come back, don't worry about it," with this nonchalant attitude. I still continue to look for him everywhere, I looked under the bed, down the street, at all my friends' houses, I called his friends, his girlfriend's house, I even looked in closets and he was still missing.

My mom hadn't gotten home from work yet. I knew right then and there that he didn't give a rat's ass about

Michael coming home or not. He was only worried about getting high and finding something else to pawn. So by this time it was around 10:00PM and my mother had just made it home from work and I told her everything that was going on. I already had called all his friends and my friends and no one had heard from him since earlier that day around 5:00PM. So my mother decided to go and look for him. She looked through the house and she even went through the neighborhood. When it was past 11:00PM she started looking in the trash cans in the dark and rainy alley all alone, with no help from Bug, all he did was continue to lay in the bed and look like a stoned zombie in the face. My mom didn't want to think of the worse but she had to, that's why she looked in the trash cans because of the lady that was found dead in the garbage can a month prior, right outside of our house. Someone had stuffed her lifeless body in a trash bin and folded her body in a backwards U. It was a scene from the movies and an image that you never want to see as a kid. She looked and looked and Michael was nowhere to be found. So she finally made it in the house around 1:00am and checked the house again from top to bottom and Michael was still nowhere to be found. She then started to clean up the house because when my mom was stressed she cleaned and while she was cleaning up she found that she had a lot of bags that needed to be recycled. This was the only place she didn't look because it was so dark and scary back there, so she took the bags of paper into the back room in the basement and as she reached to cut on the light she discovered a gruesome discovery. My brother's lifeless body hanging from a pole by a shoe string that wrapped around his neck. His body wasn't facing the front, so my mom had to turn her son around to see that he was dead and it was really her baby hanging up there dead while his eyes were wide open and his tongue hanging out of his mouth. His feet were still inches away from the ground still able to get down if he wanted to.

I think after that her life changed before her eyes. She just saw her only son hanging soulless and helpless. That really was too much for her to handle. My mother screamed and screamed and when I heard her I came from my room upstairs and ran halfway down the stairs to see my stepfather at the bottom of the stairs sitting across the last step punching the wall and screaming no-no-no-no and my mother was in the back room yelling call the police, call the police. I immediately ran upstairs to call the police.

"Hello, 911. Yes, my mom is yelling and screaming and she told me to call the police, hurry, hurry!!" I yelled frantically. When I got off of the phone my heart fell out of my chest because I knew then what happened. It took calling 911 to realize what really was happening. I proceeded to run out of the house in just a tee shirt yelling and screaming, "My brother, no,no,no my brother is dead, he's gone." I then ran to my friend's house and rang her door bell in shock not knowing that I had laid my finger on the door bell and it was like 5:00AM in the morning. When she opened the door I fell to my knees and begged and pleaded for GOD....

My brother is gone, I yelled!

As I am standing in her front hallway with a t-shirt, underwear and socks on. Still not really understanding what really is going on because I still have not had confirmation that he was really gone. I still didn't even realized that I had no clothes on either. I was literally out of my mind. I ran out of the house with what I was sleep in. After that moment I knew my life would never be the same again.

Michael and I were very close and we confided in each other as well as told each other everything. Michael and I knew more than we should have known or even seen at that age, but we did and this is my thought: This is ONLY MY PERSONAL THOUGHT, no legal evidence has been proven. I strongly feel that my brother DID NOT commit suicide and that someone ELSE is responsible for my brother's death.

He never did like my brother and he always would get into it with him and fight with him. He didn't like the fact that my mother would do any and everything for her children, especially for Michael because he was a diabetic and he needed special attention. He also didn't hide it either, him and my mother would fight all the time about what she did for her kids and how spoiled we were and didn't deserve half of the things that she did for us. She would always have black eyes and me and my brother would always hear them fight because we were in the next room from them. My sister slept upstairs from us, so she was always to herself all the time. We heard the fights and hitting and all of that. Me and my brother would sit in the room and hold each other and cry. We were scared and never knew what to do, so we would cry all night and wake up the next morning and look at him in disgust and be mad and would always talk with each other about how we felt about their relationship.

I strongly feel that my brother Michael didn't kill himself. He actually had a lot going on. My brother was about to graduate from 8th grade with me, so he was very excited about that. We had plans for the summer and we promised each other that we would never leave each other, no matter what.

Two days after my brother's funeral Bug went through my brother's things and took all of his electronics and pawned them all. This wasn't the first time that our things were pond or stolen. We would sometimes get out things back and sometimes we didn't. All we was told was don't worry about he go give it back. My mother was still blind to the fact that her boyfriend was on drugs and she still stayed with him. Is this ok? I didn't really understand at all.

The medical examiner returned Michael's belongs that were on his body at the time of the discovery. We found a note in his pocket that said (Find me in the storage room hanging). I started wondering that if this was a suicide note it wouldn't be in his pocket on him while he hung himself, he would have at least left it for someone to find it. My family did their own investigation – they found out that my intuition was right. The note that was found in my brother's pocket matched up to the hand writing of the devil himself! We are no investigators, but we did have the knowledge to decipher whose handwriting it was. The letter that was in my brother's pocket was compared to everyone's handwriting in that house as well as friends. This information was never told before. This all happened after my brother was buried and they said to re-open the case – we would have to exhume his body and it would cost $5,000.00 to do that and to bury him again it would be another $5,000.00 that my mother said she didn't have. My opinion; if it was me I would have spent my last money if I even had a feeling or thought that someone that I was dating for over 10 years was a possible suspect in the death of my son. I would sell my soul if I had too. Everyone doesn't think like I do. But she still stayed with him after that, and at this point I was really scared for my life. I started to run away and be around boys, gangs, and drugs. I felt that the people on the streets cared more about me then my own mother did and I was protected from the devil himself.

It was now one month after my brother's death and it was time for me to graduate, and all I could think about was that my brother was supposed to be graduating too and we had plans to go to high school. I was so numb to everything. I remember walking across the stage but can't seem to remember anything else. This was all I could think about on my graduation day.... That I really didn't care about anything.

VENTING:

I can remember the times my brother Michael and I had our bad times together, he hit me in the eye with a hard ice ball and it made my eye close. Michael was definitely bad sometimes. He made me put my thumb in the crack of the door and then slammed it and my entire nail came off. He used to burst through my door all the time to break the lock because that's what he did, he was very over protective of me ... until one day I was tired of it so we played a game of dare and I dared him to put crazy glue on his penis and let it dry, and of course we were dare devils and tried everything once but I wanted to get him back for all the bad things he used to do to me. He did it. It really worked and two hours passed and he could not pee at all even though it felt like he had to go to the restroom the glue was taking longer than I could imagine for it to wear off. He had to stand in front of the toilet for six hours

Hurt Used To Live Here

before it wore off. He even tried to peel it off until it started to bleed. That was actually funny because he did more to me in my 13 years of life than I did to him, but I know it was love because me and my brother looked out for each other during the good and bad times.

It sounds all bad but what I would do to get all that back. He one day dared me to crazy glue all my fingers together and I did. Then my mom came home early as I was trying to undo all my fingers, but couldn't and ended up peeling some of my skin off my fingers, I ended up getting in trouble. There was also a time when my brother called me to the back door and as I leaned to look out to see where he was he pushed me and I fell down 6 stairs, all I did was jump right back up and act like nothing even happened. I was a tom boy because my brother made me rough. We were something like the show jackass. I even heard that he used to play with fire a lot and that he was kind of upset that I came into the picture because he was the baby until I arrived home from the hospital and he waited until I was in my crib and set it on fire while I was still in it. I was actually too young to remember but my mom told me the story. There was a time when I was in my walker and he pushed me down 18 basement stairs and I landed straight up at the end of my fall! I can now laugh about it because I miss him so much and if the abuse, fun times and dares, is what I have to remember I can only imagine if his life wasn't taken at fifteen I would have a lot more to write about.

He was my best friend,
my brother,
and my world!

The turnaround:

When I finally got to High School I really thought I was going to go crazy – I had deaths in my family and I thought that GOD was punishing our family for allowing this to happen to us. I really didn't know what was going on. My life was over and I didn't have anyone else in my life that I could call a family. My friends saw it and as well as my mother because she knew the pain and anger that I felt with her, all of that was overwhelming for me. I was failing my grades in school and being more and more to myself. I was quiet and stayed to myself. I started to cut my classes to find attention from doing other things. I started to drink and smoke weed and hang out all types of the nights.

Until one day my mother had a teacher parent's conference with one of my teachers to find out what was going on with me. She explained to them that I was going through a lot and that I was not well. She told them that I had experienced a lot of deaths and that I was emotionally stressed out and didn't know how to handle it. To make the long story short, they lied on me to my mom and she didn't defend me so I did, I took up for myself and got kicked out of high school. There was this thing that if you got in any trouble at school, we had to roll a dice and get hit with a paddle on the hands as many times as the dice rolled on it. Not on my watch were you going to hit me and think it was ok. At that time I blamed my mom because she didn't fight for me or even defend me at all even if I was right. All this time I thought this is what she has always been giving me. Why am I shocked now? I had something far worse happening in my life.

Hurt Used To Live Here

In Loving Memory Of

Michael Allen Collins-Reed

Wednesday, May 22, 1996

Visitation: 11:00 A.M. Service: 12:00 P.M.

Gatling's Chapel
10133 South Halsted Street
Chicago, Illinois 60628

Prophet Joseph Bailey • *Officiating*

Joyce Reed

FOUR

Chapter 4

THE STRUGGLE

I was a little girl when you thought it was ok to touch me in that private place. When I was around 9 years old we used to have so many people in and out of our house that I couldn't keep up with them all. We had family, friends, neighborhood kids, step kids, and cousins living with us. I enjoyed it because I was never bored, but what I didn't enjoy was the late nights when a family member used to come into my room and fondle me and try to put his fingers in places that they wasn't allowed to go at 9. I remember it happening several times until it started to hurt really bad. I used to have to hide my panties because they would have crust and yellowish stains in them all the time. I knew it wasn't normal but I couldn't tell my mom and have her worrying about me especially when she had a million other things to do. It went on for a couple of years on May Street until the next time he came into my room to fondle me.

The night in question he actually wanted to go further and partake in make believe sex acts and as he crept in my room and tried to touch me. I yelled and said "leave me alone, you're hurting me." No one even heard me, not even my mom and she was 2 doors away in her bedroom. The only thing that was separating us was a wall and a bathroom. Maybe because I had a very soft voice or was it because no one ever cared. The most important thing is that he stopped. I never mentioned it to anyone because for what? Was something going to be done about it or was anyone going to even listens or believe me? Today I am speaking out about it not to hurt anyone but to release it all to get past it and move on for me. I have been holding on to this for years and I can't continue to let it affect my life. I have to release, Let go and Let God!

Protect Me:

My life was like a box of chocolates – I never knew what I was going to get. Not even a week after my grandmother "Glo" died I ended up writing my mom this letter:

Dear Mommy,
Today I woke up late, and had to rush. As I leave out for school to try to catch 2 buses that rode right pass me. I stood on the bus stop waiting and stomping my feet because of the time and I knew I was going to be late for my 1st and second period class. I didn't want to be late again – I stand there and as I look for the next bus, who do I see, Yes! I see my friend's stepfather pulling up in his white van. I get in the car with a huge weight lifted off my shoulders; I will make it to school on time. Mommy he had different plans he asked if he can pay me $10 to touch me. If I did let him I couldn't tell anyone because I would mess up his marriage and he would only touch me only if it was okay. He tried to offer me the new Jordan gym shoes and other things. I was so scared at this point so as he comes to a stop light I jump out of the car and walk the rest of the way to school. Mommy please don't say anything to my friend I don't want anyone to be mad at me. Between me and you.
Love Red

Hurt Used To Live Here

Joyce Reed

"Red was a nickname that the guys from the neighborhood called me." for clarification.

This happened with one of my friend's step dad on 10/28/1996 to be exact. The reason why I told my mom not to say anything was because I didn't want to lose a great friend and nothing happened I thought it wasn't a big deal. That is what I thought. Then what happened on 10/3/1994 was the reason I never said anything else if something was to have happened to me.

I am so tired:

One day I went to my mother and told her that I didn't like the fact that my (stepfather) was hitting on her and making her look ugly. I said that she deserve better because every time she comes home he fusses at her and fights her all the time. I was tired of him hitting us too all the time and him thinking that he was my dad. If it wasn't for what my dad did, he wouldn't be putting his hands on me. My step-dad was scared of my dad so he took full advantage when my dad wasn't in my life. When we thought that my stepdad was on drugs we told mom and then told her not to say a thing and not to even mention it to him. He was always so quick to say whip their ass! After all of that was said I thought it would be a perfect opportunity to tell her how I felt about her not caring about her children any more. My mom was working so she didn't have time for her kids anymore – my mom was not a conversational person at all – and if you needed something you would be better off leaving a note on her dresser. She usually leaves the reply on the bathroom mirror for you to see when we got ready for school or if you got up to use the bathroom in the middle of the night. My mom looked at me with this sad look that made me feel sorry for her. Still not understanding why I felt bad and she was hurting us and we weren't hurting her. When I wanted to know what to do with this maxi-pad when blood came from my vagina? Why am I bleeding? Why do I need to wear this thing around my chest? It's very uncomfortable to me. Why you never gave me a hug and told me that you love me? I was alone in the inside and it hurts even more not being able to really understand WHY? Before my brother even died – my stepfather would steal my things out of my room and pawn them and when I would tell my mother about what he was doing – she would say that it wasn't true or when she knew he took things, she would justify his actions by saying he would give it back to me if he did take it. I told my mom that he was doing Drugs and that he would pawn our things for drugs, that why our things would come up missing all the time. I knew he did because my uncles were on drugs as well and he would hang out with them all the time and they would steal from our family all the time they never hid it and when that started to happen I knew that he was on drugs too. They stole anything that wasn't tied down. CD's, radios, televisions, jewelry, even my granny coins that she collected for many years. It was a point where I thought my clothes would come up missing too. It was so bad that I started to write down all my things to see what was missing and what came back, if it did come back.

You Piece of SHIT:

I remember clearly when I was in the 7th grade and just got transferred to a new school in the neighborhood. That alone was stressful for me because I have been going to the same school since

Joyce Reed

4th grade and to take me out at 7th grade to meet new people was traumatizing to me. I did end up transferring back to my old school and graduate with all my friends.

This was nothing new that my brother Michael and I always got in trouble and were on punishment, but I can't remember what we did to get on punishment this time. All I knew was that my father said that we had to work with him to get off punishment. This was a perfect opportunity to get off punishment and go to my friend's sleepover. My brother said that he would stay on punishment but I wanted to do what I had to do to go to my friend's sleepover so I went to work with him. My father worked at the flea market every Saturday and Sunday faithfully selling different things from a lawn mower, tools DVD, clothes, to furniture and cars. I was already confident that I could do this and get home in enough time to go to my friend's sleepover. I had seen him do this so many times that I knew I would pick up fast. How hard is it to ask a customer what they want and get it for them and take the money? I had this routine down packed because I would see him do it all the time. He would also have us working at his popcorn shop off of 79th and Cottage Grove on the weekends if we wanted extra money. I was already used to dealing with people and customers.

On this day I agreed to spend the night with him on Friday and get up and go to work on Saturday. He goes to the Flea market like 3:00am so if I was already with him all I had to do was get up and work to get the day over with. My father picked me up from my mom's house Friday night and we headed up to my little sister's house to pick her up so that I could have someone to play with and talk to. I never spent the night alone at my daddy's house; because I knew it would be boring. So as we were heading to my sister's house we drove down the block and my father rode right past her house and he never stopped. He just rode past and said that she wasn't there. I felt it was a little strange but all I cared about was getting off punishment and having fun at my friend's sleepover, nothing else mattered. Why didn't he stop at her house? I asked myself. I never went over to my daddy's house without one of my sisters or my brother there with me so I'm like I will be bored as hell. My father told me that he needed to make another stop before we headed home. We stopped by his friend's house for a second because my daddy was going out of town that weekend and his friend had gotten his suit out of the cleaners earlier that morning for him.

It was actually October 1994 and I think he was going to go to Las Vegas with my step mom, that's why he needed the suit. While we were at his friend's house I went upstairs to the bathroom. I can remember that the hall ways were dark and narrow and I had to feel my way through that house. As I was coming down the stairs from the bathroom I heard my father and his friend talking about something but the only thing that I heard was, "you better get some before you leave." Those 7 words were the only words that stuck out as I was walking down the basement stairs to meet my father. It was an awkward silence and strange looks, but I was so tired that I just wanted to get out of there and go back to sleep, by now its 1:00AM in the morning. He sits me on his lap, like always and tells me to give him a kiss.

"Come on baby, let's go home, he said."

We left and went back to my daddy's basement apartment on 82th and Prairie. It was cold and smelled just like a basement too. This was my first time there, let alone being there by myself. I was always used to going over my step-mothers house. It was dark and had bars on all the windows and 2 to 3 dead bolts locks on each door, with no door knobs at all. The bathroom was small but he made it work. He made one side out of his space and the other side for my little sisters that would sometimes come and visit.

My father and step mother were separated at the time, so that's why my father was living in a basement apartment. As we got settled and ready for bed I wanted to watch a bootleg "my father was the bootleg king he had all the new movies." I picked the new nightmare with Freddie. I put on my favorite pajamas that my mom had got me the year before for Christmas. It was all white with red strips short set. My sister and I had the same set but she had all red with white strips in it. As I was lying down, he asked me do I like pillows and I would have to share one with him, if I wanted a pillow? I looked with the awkward face and said sure.

We laid down and fell asleep together as we watched New Nightmare. It was around 4 or 5:00AM when I woke up to my daddy feeling and rubbing on my butt and my chest but he never said a word to me so I thought he was dreaming and I never wanted to open my eyes to see that this was real and that this was really happening to me. It was the scariest thing that has happened thus far in my life, and all I could keep in my head was that this nightmare I was having and that it was definitely a dream. He began to take my bottoms off and he unbuttoned my top and put me on top of him and tried to penetrate me, and I was only 12 so I was a virgin and I didn't even know what was really happening. He pushed and pushed until he had his way with me. I was scared as hell because this was my daddy and I feared him. He had sex with me and without me even saying a word or making any movements. I kept my eyes closed the entire time but peeked to see if I wasn't really dreaming and this was really happening to me by the hands of my own father. He went on and on until I felt something wet and sticky all over me. When he was done, he got up and laid me on the bed and he got in the shower. Still not saying a word to me.

While he was in the shower I put my pajamas back on and tried to find a way out but he had all the dead bolts locked on his doors. I finally found his keys on the messy dresser. There were like 200 keys on one ring. He had keys like a janitor at your school. I went to the door and tried like 10 keys on each lock of the door, and then went to the back door and tried another 10 keys on those locks too. I was scared and shaking then I heard the water turning off so I jumped back in the bed and I acted like I was still asleep. He walked up to me and shook me and told me to get up and get in the shower but I still was pretending that I was asleep. He waited for a second and realized that I was asleep and he came and sat on the bed and laid me across his lap and said that he was sorry, and that he didn't mean to do that to me, he didn't know what he was thinking and he loved me so much as he rubbed my head. My daddy went on to say that I could have anything that I wanted and never to tell anyone. After a while of my just laying there iin disgust and disbelief. I finally got up, got in the shower and put my clothes on without saying one word to him and we remain like nothing happened, I helped him load the truck and on to work.

There was times when I thought about just running when I finally got out from behind those bars in that smelly basement apartment. I thought about getting a knife and stabbing him to death. I also thought about screaming for my life but I was so afraid of him that I just pretended that nothing happened like he told me to do and went on to work with him. We were actually on 47th and Ashland in Chicago at the flea market and I remember seeing

Joyce Reed

a McDonald's there so I asked him if I could get something to eat so he gave me some money to get something to eat but instead of eating I called my mommy on the pay phone and told her that I didn't feel good, and I wanted to go home, and if she could meet me on 79th and Ashland? I was too scared to even tell her because I was already scared of my father so I didn't say anything at all to her. I did cry to her on the phone but just told her that my stomach was hurting. She then told me that if my stomach was hurting then get on the bus going south bound and she would meet on 79th and Ashland bus stop.

"Mommy, I don't know how to catch the bus."

She said, "Were is your dad?"

I told her that he was still working and too busy to stop just to take me home.

I then decided that I would just stay there and stick it out because I didn't want her to call my dad and I get a whooping. I hung up the phone and went back to work with him. The day seemed like it would never end, until the day actually ended finally. We packed up what was left of what he didn't sell and he took me home. On the way home, he wanted to make it clear that if I told anyone that I would be in big trouble and I would get a whooping. My dad's whoopins were more like a beating. If we got in trouble we had to write 5000 lines and have all our brothers and sisters hit us with the belt and then him.

I recall a beating that I got on the day of my brother funeral that left a scar on my calf for years. That's all I could think of as he threatens me not to say anything to anybody EVER! He said that he would give me whatever I wanted if I didn't say anything. He knew I loved money so he gave me $200.00 in cash and I got out of the car after giving him a kiss on the lips. I felt like I won the lottery. I never held $200 cash in my hand expecially at 12years old.

It felt so good to reach that porch at home that all I wanted to do was take a shower and go to bed. I didn't even go to my friend's sleepover.

I would ask him for money just because blackmail can get you anything you want and I was a teenager with a shopping habit. What was I to do? My father had me scared and would tell me that he would beat me if I told someone even though he knew what he did to me was wrong and shouldn't have happened. What was I to do? Who would care anyway? This wasn't the first time this happened to me. I didn't tell anyone then. I just wrote everything down in my journals and note book. My mother had other things to worry about like getting beat up every day and her own life. I felt my problems would only steer her from her pain and focus on me but I wanted her to see that the man she was with was no good.

Now my mother would wonder where I got a large amount of money from and I couldn't explain.

I stayed in silence until 3 months went by. January 8, 1995 I wrote her a letter telling her what had happened in detail. I even went on to say "I think he spremed in me." I was not ashamed of what I was writing to my mom at all. I told her everything in that letter. She immediately took me to the ER to get checked out. She was very upset because I never said anything. I went to the doctor and they examined me for hours and asked me a thousand questions. I was questioned by the police, case workers, doctors, nurse assistants, and the whole nine yards. I eventually had to get a pap smear and it was very painful. They asked me did he ejaculate in me and I didn't really know, but I did feel some slimy stuff on my vagina I told the doctor. I told them that he made me get in the shower right after too.

Dark Secret:

There is a deep dark secret that no one knows about the case. Between October, 1994 and January, 1995, that I went silent. I found out that I was pregnant and had to keep this from EVERYONE. OH MY GOD, my own biological father got me pregnant and my mom had her problems and her religion didn't agree with aborting a baby, so I just took matters into my own hands. When I later found out that I was pregnant. I did what I knew how to do and that was to hustle to get the money for an abortion, or kill it myself. I didn't need much because my father gave me money every week. I didn't care what I had to do to get rid of this demon in my stomach. I couldn't tell my family because some of them are very judgmental and would never understand or believe me anyway. I looked and searched high and low until I met this lady that advised me to take a few packs of birth control pills and it would end my pregnancy. What else did I have to lose? I already had the money so I paid her to get the pills and a week later I miscarried. I was using the bathroom one day and as I was peeing in the toilet I had to urge to push, I pushed and pushed and plopped in the toilet water there was a cloudy circular ball floating in the toilet. You could see the fetus and the veins on the baby. I was scared and didn't know what to do but to flush the toilet and to move on with my life. It was so little, it was the size of a golf ball. I decided to pick it up to get a closer look at it. You could actually see the baby forming. I squeezed it and flush it.

Whew, I finally got that off my chest! Yes my life was fucked up, I know it!!

I'm still trying to figure out WHY ME at this point??

I had to end up going from courthouse to courthouse and seeing different doctors and talking to various therapists. I was scared for my life because my father always beat us for no reason and he would leave marks on us that were permanent. So after going to court over and over he never showed up. That's because he knew what he did and he couldn't face me or my mother. He moved out of that building that next weekend because the police went to the apartment and they said when he had moved out which a week after the incident was happened.

Now, let me take you back for a second.

I have to remind you that, my father was a married man and the woman he was married to, I loved her dearly. I looked up to her like another mom. I didn't want her to think that I was ruining her marriage. I thought that she was upset with me or did she even know what was going on? So I called her up and told her what happened and she did not even believe me. She told me that I needed to come over and we all needed to sit down and talk. I thought that was a bad idea, and my own mother told me NO anyway. My step mother was in denial because that was her husband and she had two children by him. She didn't want to believe that he had done this to his own flesh and blood. I never could answer that and still to this day I am clueless about why would he do something like that to one of his children. I used to cry when I saw myself in the mirror and wondered if I was not what he wanted me to be, why did he do it to me? Was he not thinking? My daddy never smoked or drank so I knew it was not that. I had so many questions with no answers. I will never know the truth. I will never forget what he has done to me and how he has caused stress, pain and discomfort in my life. Dad you are supposed to protect your children and keep them from danger, but you did the opposite. I love you because you are my father but you made me NEVER able to EVER trust you again or anybody else. I was so happy that I had a mother like I did to support me in a time like this. She was on top of everything until oneday......

Un-Protected:

She stuck by my side and understood me until one day they dropped the case because they couldn't find him. I didn't understand the court system at all but I was like why go to all these court dates and counseling for them to just drop it like that? I was really upset with my mother at that time because I felt that she gave up on me so I give up on her and make her feel my pain. I started disrespecting her and not listening to her. Why me? I asked myself every day. Why me? I was tired of talking and listening to people that would end up disappointing me anyway. I didn't trust anyone anymore, not even my mother and that was hard for me to do. I suffered hurt and pain every day of my life and to think that if your mother would give up on you was a hurtful thing.

My mother had her own life and she had other children that she had to deal with so if she didn't give me the attention I needed then I will go out and get it. I then went through life saying and knowing: "My own father took my innocence from me and made me afraid that if someone was to ever do something to me that keeping quiet would be the best thing for me because no one would care." My father used to do harmful things to us as kids. I never thought that it was okay but who was I to tell? Who was there to tell me right from wrong? I was on my own. By that point in my

Dear Gregory A. Reed:

As you read this letter, you may need to sit down first. It has been 19 years since you ruined my life. Oct 3, 1994 was the day that has haunted me to this day. You walk around degrading people, treating people like shit, you LIE, and would even sell your soul to the devil to get what you want but GOD sees everything you do. You are a disgrace to mankind. You are the devil and GOD WILL PUNISH you for ALL you have done to EVERY-ONE especially GOD's other children because clearly you took something from every one of his children. We are supposed to be your children, but you ruined that too.

I used to pray that bad would happen to you. That you would suffer like I had to for over 19 years of my life. You took something from me that was mines, mines for safe keeping. What you did was beneath everything GOD believes in. How could you wake up every day knowing that you messed SO MANY people lives up? What you did to me will never be understood. YOU ARE A COWARD, A PUNK, A LIAR, A RAPIST, A CHILD MOLESTER, A PUSSY, A BASTARD, AN ASSHOLE, A FAGGOT, AND CAN'T FORGET A BITCH ASS NIGGA. Your day will come Greg. LOL!!! You will pay for fucking my life up and not allowing me to understand life, and how a person can do this to their own flesh and blood?? This is what you see on TV every day, not ever thinking that it would happen to me. You were supposed to protect me, watch over me, guide me in the right direction, teach me about boys, growing up, what to watch out for instead you did the opposite, you are a coward and you took my innocence from me when I was 11 years old and never was fucking man enough to admit it to not only me but to the people that think you are normal. GREG TURN AND LOOK AT YOUR DAUGHTER?!?!?!?!? SHE IS AROUND THE SAME AGE I WAS WHEN YOU HAD SEX WITH ME…… I KNOW, LOOK AT HER, SHE IS SO INNOCENT AND PRECIOUS, ISNT SEE????

Why was I the one that had to be ruined? You should have been locked up behind bars but instead you ran like a coward and never faced the truth… How do you feel after looking at her??? What are you feeling???

You never once came to me and said you were sorry, you never explained how and why you did what you did? Not just to me but all of your children you raped, molested, fondled, have rubbed you or kissed or got pregnant Instead you tried to make me out to be the bad person, talked down about me and told people that I was a hoe and slut and prostitute. How could you say those things about your own flesh and blood? But in the same breath you are raping and doing GOD knows what with you OWN….. I heard from 3 of your daughters that you molested them too, but they haven't exposed you like I have.

You left ALL of your children to run up behind a woman that is half your age… You are not stable at all. You have kids, rape them, and leave and move on to the next, smh!!! You hurt people for enjoyment. Its time everyone laughs at you.

I'm writing you this letter because its time I share my story to the world to help others get through the pain after rape, betrayal, neglect and being fatherless. My book is in the making and will be published soon and ALL your LIES will come out for the world

Hurt Used To Live Here

to see. Your beautiful, so called life will never be the same, as I haven't been the same since Oct 3, 1994.

I used to ask this question to myself all the time? WHY DOES GOD keep allowing you to have girls for you to fondle, rape, and molest??? I just don't understand AT ALL. Its time you deal with everything I was forced to deal with ALL MY LIFE!!!!! I want you to know that it still hurts me to this day and I am still hurt for what you have done to me…… I had to forgive you, only because that what GOD says to do. But I will NEVER FORGET!!!!

Greg, No one fucking likes you and never will. You are living through the devils world but GOD is bigger than him and he will show you in due time. SPEAK NOW OR FOREVER HOLD YOUR PEACE, GREG!!!! Be a man and turn to everyone and tell them who you really are: Child molester, rapist, fondler, faggot, beater, and liar.

Tell everyone that you use to BEAT us until we bleed, you made us rub your feet daily, you made us kiss you in the mouth, you made us write 1,000's of lines until or fingers were numb, you use to play Russian roulette with us and laugh about it. Now it's my time I play Russian runlet with your life. You will be exposed to the world. Maybe you can finally know what it feels like to want to die, end your life, and be ashamed and embarrassed. Maybe finally you can just put everyone out of their misery and just shot yourself in the fucking face and deal with your father "the devil" he is waiting on you… Whatever your plans are, I hope you are man enough to accept the outcome. Even if you decide to still not say anything and continue you're so called wonderful life, you will be exposed. I will ruin the rest of your life you have on this earth.

Hurt Used To Live Here

I will posts signs telling everyone to beware that a child molester lives right next door, beware that you are less than 2 miles from a daycare.... It's my time to smile again.
If you decide to end your life, I will be at your funeral telling my story there. Either way I will hunt you down until you grow some balls and speak the REAL TRUTH
You owe SOOOOOOOOO many people but most of all you owe ME!!!!
That eye of yours is just the beginning of your punishment; he has more in store for you.... I PROMISE!!!

Sincerely,
Your worst nightmare

Hurt Used To Live Here

life I thought that no one cared about my little issues , that's why I grew up to be by myself and alone. I never felt loved or wanted.

After 19 years I have the courage to write my dad "the sperm donor" a letter (to the left) and this is what the letter said:

When I wrote this letter to my "sperm donor" it was a relief and a weight lifted off my shoulders, because people needed to be aware of what they were living next door to and I needed him to feel my pain. I mailed it to his house so he would know that what he did was wrong and I never forgot about that day and that day has haunted me for a long time. I used every vile and vulgar word I could think of, every despicable phrase or anecdote that I knew, to describe what I thought of him and his actions. Calling him a coward was the least offensive word that I could call him. Much of what I said was my own feeble attempt at striking back at him, for I was defenseless otherwise.

The saddest part of this story is that the rape from my father was just the beginning of men taking advantage of me sexually.

Fed Up:

It didn't go as planned one day as I went to my crush's house at the time. A friend and I were dating best friends that we used to hang out, drink, and talk shit with. Yes drink! I was actually drinking and smoking when I was 13. It wasn't a big deal and my mom let her boyfriend give us beer telling us that it killed the worms. I was drinking Hennessey and smoking weed. I thought that I was cool at that time. I was just trying to fit in and it was hard not having parents to guide me and teach me about temptation and

Joyce Reed

persuasion. Instead everything that I learned today was learned from books, TV, friends, streets, and just seeing it in real life. No guidance at all! If I could change it I would, but it really wasn't a cool thing to do at all.

One day in particular me and my friend walked over to her boyfriends' house to hang out and she wanted to have sex. She was older than me and having sex already. I was scared due to my past and the pain of it all, it hurt so badly. I guess this is when he got fed up. After my friend was done doing the do with her boyfriend we went outside and hung out on the porch for a while. I realized I should go and pee before we went on our way back home, walking. I went back in to their mom's house and went in to use the bathroom. "Joyce", my male crushed yelled from upstairs.

"Joyce come here for a second."

After drying my hands I ran upstairs thinking something was wrong, from the tone of his voice. I walked in the room to find him sitting on the bed just staring at me. I stood at the door and behind the door was a closet. As I walked closer to the bed to him the closet door was being pushed opened closing the door to the room. My male crush, Bull was his name, was still sitting on the bed and my friend's boyfriend was the one busting out of the closet door. My boy crush then grabbed me and said,

"You gone give me this pussy."

Bull threw me on the bed and ripped my black shorts off while his friend had his knees in my arms over my head and his right hand over my mouth and his left hand touching me while Bull had his way with me. It lasted like about 10 minutes but felt like 15 hours. I got my mouth free and bit him so hard and screamed and ran outside in tears to where my friend was. I knew that I was safe then but to my surprise the first thing that I hear from her was,

"BITCH YOU JUST FUCKED MY MAN!"

I knew then that I was alone again. It seemed like every time something so devastating happened to me everyone turned their back on me like I asked for it. Why did everyone hate me? I didn't have anyone to talk to, vent to, or even hold me and tell me that everything would be ok. The only person I had was me, myself and I. After the 4th time my body was violated I was through with men. I was going to do whatever I had to do to treat all men like they treated me. It only got worse from here. I began to drink and party more. I only had a hand full of friends because it was very hard for me to trust anyone in life. I had no remorse. No feeling in my entire body. I just didn't care if I lived or died. Who would care anyway? I was hanging out in the streets more, getting involved with gangs, and dealing drugs. I even had a gun, a little 22. I felt that I didn't protect me who was?

I felt like everyone in my family was against me. It felt like I was living a dream world and one day I was going to wake up to a real family that really loved me. I always prayed for a different family, and hoping that I was adopted. After my mom told me that when she was pregnant with me – she wanted to abort me and my dad came in and grabbed her out of the office. I wish she would have gone through with the process because my family was fucked up mentally. That was my only way out of this crazy family. So until I was free and away from them. I did more and more wrong.

UNEXPECTED:

My friends and I met these guys that had a big crib and when we needed to get away with no worries that was the place to be. It was huge, like a mini mansion, their parents was always traveling so we had the house to ourselves.

This was the last day that I drank dark liquor. We played the questions game.

It's a drinking game where you have to go around in a circle and ask questions to each other. You couldn't answer the questions but replied with another question to the person that asked you the question in the first place, and it goes on until someone messed up and gets drunk. Oh Lord! I was the first one drunk! I remember passing out from being so drunk. When I came to, I woke up to 5 naked men in the same room that I was asleep in. I was also naked too. I didn't know what to do at this point because I was in and out of it. I remember feeling my body in so much pain and when I finally woke up and sat up everyone had ran out of the room except the guy I was talking to. I asked him what happened and he said nothing we just had sex. I said why were they all in here and he brushed me off by saying something that I don't even remember. I got up and told my friends lets go. I went home again and took a 2 hour shower,

I was like DAMN #5, what the hell was going on? This time I'm not saying anything to anyone about this. I felt angry and hurt again .How can a man do this to a woman that is passed out and her body is limp? What do you get out of that? Is it exciting to you? How did I get here anyway? Where are my friends? What's going on? These are all the questions that were going through my head at once. It only made me hate men even more.

Final Straw:

It was a total of 7 times in my life that I was raped, fondled or violated by different men, or more than once by the same person. Enough was enough for me. The last man that raped me had been my last straw and he had no idea what I was feeling and what I've been through at all. After he had his way with me after forcing himself on me. I waited until he went to sleep and pulled his pants down. All men think that when a woman pulls their pants down it's time for them to relax and get some head, but no not this time! I gently rubbed his penis until it got hard and grabbed my ink pen and took the cover off and just exposed the ink filter. I whispered in his ear so softly and said baby are you ready for this? He said in his sexy voice, "Yes baby" and he grabbed my head and pushed it towards his penis because he was ready for this good head! As he grabbed my head I grabbed his dick with my right hand and with the left hand I jabbed the pen so far in his penis that he jumped up and tried to swing on me. I went for my gun that was in my purse and put the gun to his head and told him that if he told anyone that I would kill him. I always had a gun around with me and you would never know especially around men. It was never loaded because with so much anger and pain built up I might have just killed someone. I never loaded my gun. It just felt good saying those words to someone else. That's all I heard all my life so it felt good to me. I got my things and never looked back.

No Idea:

I was a red bone with a really nice shape – I had big "C" cups with a little waist and big legs and no booty of course. I had hazel brown eyes that changed colors during the seasons that turned so many people on. I just went along with it. I even was asked crazy questions in regard to them.

Damn baby your eyes are grey today, do you feel those changing colors? REALLY fool?

They had no idea what they were getting themselves into dealing with me. I was their worst nightmare waiting to get off on their ass. I never got the chance to know what real sex from a man felt like. It was always taken, painful, and or dry to me. I would always wish they would hurry up so I can go eat or go get my nails done. It wasn't enjoyable like women say it was. I would always look at them and was like.

Ugh you nasty!

Even when I had a boyfriend that I loved dearly it wasn't painful but it wasn't all that enjoyable either. It was like a hurry up or let me get a nut off. A man never made me have an orgasm, so I never felt that passion in sex at all, let alone with a man. All I knew was that men were dogs, hoes, players, tramps, manipulators, violators, pushovers, sex talkers, sex getters, users and perverts. Why, you ask? Because that's all I've seen! Try to prove me wrong so I can prove you right!

The Facts:

Women you can be with a man for years or months, but when you say no and they disregard what you say and still attempt to get what they want it is the definition of rape! Anything that is taken from you without permission is rape and your body should never be violated.

Hurt Used To Live Here

Tell someone!

If your family doesn't listen, go to a close friend. If you can't pick up a phone and call an abuse hotline – they are anonymous. Get the help you need and report it ASAP! Getting raped is not your fault. You didn't deserve it. A woman can walk outside half naked but that doesn't give anyone the right to take advantage of her. They're messed up in the head, not you! The first step is telling someone that will help.

Joyce Reed

FIVE

Chapter 5

MOTHERHOOD AT 15

It was December of 1996, I was 14 years old and my friend KeKe and I were at my house watching TV. My sister's best friend came in and asked if we had any money and if we wanted to go to IHOP to get some breakfast. It was like 11:30PM and we were like yeah so we went to IHOP and got something to eat too. While we were eating we saw some boys on the other side of the restaurant. They were cute and my sister was looking at this high yellow boy. My other play sister was looking at his friend Buzzy, and me and my friend were just there laughing with each other. We just sat back and chilled. The guys eventually came over to our table and talked to all of us. We all had a great conversation and laughed and cracked jokes until it was like 2AM, then we finally went home. They all exchanged numbers and a couple of weeks later the guys were invited over by my sisters and when they came they brought more friends with them. One of his other friends named Cocoa came with him and I must admit that I liked him. He was 18 at the time and dark just like I liked them. Black almost blue! The drinking made him look like Denzel. I was drunk as hell and I was lying in my bed laid out and I felt someone behind me and he pulled my shorts down so fast. I didn't even get a chance to do anything. I told him to stop and move, but I didn't want to be too loud because my other sister "Lil Bit" was asleep next to me with Buzzy in the bed too. He didn't even put it all the way in and he was humping fast and I didn't even feel anything really, it happened so fast I was trying to push him away but he didn't care at all. I felt nasty because I didn't even know him like that and he took advantage of me and didn't care. All he wanted was a nut. I felt like I was being taken advantage of and I never said anything to anyone and kept it to myself. I kept telling him to stop and he didn't listen and kept going. It lasted for like 2-3 minutes but felt like forever. I got up that next morning and I was really upset and didn't really say anything to him or anyone. I just told him to leave. I didn't talk to him again until I had to. "You can know a guy and deal with a guy and if a woman says NO and the man continues without the woman's consent then that is considered rape. I can't say this enough!"

Like Normal:

I went on with my day like any other day. My thing was who will care? So keep it to yourself. It was a Saturday so I kicked it with my girls that day because we didn't have to go to school until Monday. We got something else to drink, some MD 20/20 the green flavor, and we kicked it in the neighborhood and smoked some weed. It was me, KeKe, and my best friend Nikki. We would always be together getting into stuff. Nikki was my 2nd half after my brother passed.

I was cutting classes, drinking more, and kicking it! But not focusing on what was more important and I didn't want to hear what my mother was saying. My mother was only trying to look out for me and be a mother and I ignored her and I wish she was stricter than what she was. It's like she would give up. I feel if she was more into her kids and not always working and having every man she meet take care of us while she worked things perhaps would have turned out differently. She was never there for us and she always had to work. She never told us that she loved us and she never hugged us and showed us how she felt. So when you don't have a mother there all the time to tell you right from wrong then you will feel lost and not focused on the important things. My mother was going through a tough time with losing all of her loved ones like her mother, father, her auntie, her cousin that she probably thought her family had fallen apart. Everyone was leaving us right before our eyes and it was a hard situation to deal with and I tried to understand but I was too hurt. I really didn't know what to think and don't know what was going on in my life. All I knew was that everything negative that could happen to a person in their lifetime had happened to me. I have seen it on TV but I would have never thought that it would be a part of my life.

Looking:

By the time I was fifteen I looked for something that I didn't have in my life and that was love and looking for love in all the wrong places. I looked for it from men and I thought that it was alright for a man to beat you because my mother always thought it was alright.

My 15th birthday in 1997 was like any other day to me. A happy birthday and a couple gifts and that was it. I was more in the streets that I didn't care about a birthday. I didn't feel different at all, or even strange at all. I was so detached from reality and with myself that I didn't even realize that I didn't even have a period for 3 months. I went to the doctor and she told me I was pregnant and the doctor asked me what I wanted to do. I said get rid of it. I'm only 15 years old. I told my mother that I was too young to have a baby and that I didn't want to keep it. She said because of her religion she didn't believe in abortions. She told me that she would always be there for me and that because she had lost her son within that year she wanted to replace him with my son. So I went through the pregnancy not knowing that I would be by myself and the father was nowhere to be found half the time, but if I really was looking and wanted to find him he was on 95th street selling drugs. Is this what I was going to have to deal with? I didn't want the same for my son at all. I wanted him to be the total opposite of him and go to college and be something in life other than a low life and a drug dealer. The world is not like it used to be .We can't just go chill on the porch and hang out. You need a degree to even get a job at a restaurant in some states. All I want for my son is to have a better life than me and his father did. I don't want him growing up thinking that it is ok to hang outside and sell drugs and end up getting killed or go to jail. If it was my choice I would never bring a child into this world – with the world the way it currently is. I wanted a family not just a fling I was old enough to know right from wrong but that wasn't the issue. Looking for and getting it from a low life! I was 15 and just started being a kid and seeing life. I just started getting friends and being in a happy place and I thought this (pregnancy) would ruin it. Someone actually listening and really caring was not a lot to ask for.

For all those reasons that is why I didn't want to have the baby. I begged and begged my mom to let me abort the baby because I was so young and wanted to finish school. We both agreed verbally that she would take custody of my son. How can a 15 year old take care of a baby? I told her that I was raped and didn't want my son to be in this messed up world that I lived in. I was always looking out for my unborn child, not being unselfish and trying to replace a human being. I was so confused and lost in this world that I thought your parents were supposed to guide you and protect you along the way I guess not ah? I started out being a mother at the age of 15 and had my first son because my mom made me give birth to a child that was conceived by a rape – all because she wanted to fill a void in her life because of her losing a son (Michael) months prior to that.

THIS WAS NOT IN MY PLANS:

I didn't prepare myself nor shall I say this was a huge curve ball in my life. I was always depressed and hated being pregnant. It was a hot summer in 1997 that all I seemed to eat was ice. My mom got me my own personal ice trays made just for me. Every morning I had to have a payday, ruffles cheddar chips, and a $0.25 juice. I always made sure I had $1.00. It wasn't fun and pretty like people on TV made it seem. I was getting so depressed because I had all these emotions and changes going through my body due to my pregnancy. I still hadn't gotten through all the 6 deaths in my family that incurred in the past year, nor the rapes that I was hiding and the ones that were in the open. Mind you, I was a tortured soul! I felt numb and heartless. I thought that I was dead already. I feared nothing! When I was around 5 months into my pregnancy I started to have these weird dreams that my brother Michael would be talking to me and telling me to do bad things to people because he knew what hell I was going through without him in my life.

Joyce Reed

My sister was one of the meanest sister ever. She would do mean things to us that made me and Michael really close. She tried to suffocate us with a pillow, spit in my Kool-Aid, and told me to drink it, and she dared Michael to get in the dryer and he did it but he didn't agree to her cutting it on and holding her body against the dryer door. She punched me in the eye for knocking on her door, sprayed spritz in my eyes, shall I go on? So Michael said make her pay for what she did. So I did just that when I had the perfect opportunity. I was 6 months pregnant and she used her nails and dragged them across my face and my reaction wasn't to fight because I was pregnant, but to whoop this bitch ass for all she has did to me and Michael. I did just that. My mother tried to break us up but that didn't work. I finally got tired and stopped and we went in our own rooms and shut the door. But I made sure I got at least half of my anger out on her that day. The other half would be released after our second fight when I was pregnant with my second child. My sister started to lock her bedroom door because I used to threaten her. I wanted to show her how it felt to be bullied and scared to even blink. I knew it was sibling rivalry, but I never understood why she was so mean to us and what we did to her?

Heartless:

Here comes the part where it gets deep... at 7 months pregnant I thought my feeling of not being pregnant anymore would go away but I had another thing coming. All it took was my mom thinking that she owns me just because I am doing her a favor by caring a baby that she thinks can replace her son (Michael). I always wished that I was dead and that way everyone would be better off, maybe if it was me instead of my brother than life would be better.

So I decided to attempt to end my life again. I went in the kitchen and grabbed the sharpest knife that was there and with no feeling or emotion, I went into my sister's room and stared at the mirror with the knife in my hand. I raised my shirt with my left hand and slowly went across my stomach with the knife but I couldn't do it. I really got scared when I saw a little blood. What the hell was I thinking? Was this really what I wanted to do? I just couldn't do it. At the time I was thinking of all the things my mom used to make me do, like clean my sister's room while I was 8 months pregnant and clean up after her all the time. After thinking it through very carefully, I stopped and headed to bed. I didn't know that I would have a nightmare followed by a long and rough day. My brother came to me and said to do bad things and if I didn't he would come and get me and kill me. His body was so human figured and human looking. He sat down on the edge of my bed and the crazy thing is that I felt the bed sink in from the body sitting on the bed. I convinced myself that it was really him despite the fact that Michael was actually dead. I knew that if that was my real brother he would not tell me to hurt my family let alone another human being. I was so scared that I ran so fast to my mom's room and yelled and screamed that Michael was just in my room telling me to hurt people. She said girl shut up and go to sleep. I ended up getting up the next morning so scared that I had to talk to someone. I actually went to school and talked to my counselor and she called my mom and my mom drove me to 26th and King Drive in Chicago to a mental hospital. She let them take me away at 7 ½ months pregnant. This was the start of feeling of hatefulness towards my mom.

Joyce Reed

How could you?

My mom left me in a place where I was put in a room with bars along with water bugs and mice. I knew then that love was not on my side at all. I told her that I hated her and I would never forgive her for locking me away. She knew that I had just lost 6 people in my family and dealing with a pregnancy that wasn't planned. I felt like I wanted to die all over again. How could she? How could you hear your child screaming and crying for you and all you do is walk away? She did the same thing to my brother Michael. She locked him away in a mental hospital because she couldn't deal with his real life issues. Children often take on the burdens and misplaced priorities of their parents. We were drugged up and left to talk to strangers all day. Instead of just loving and caring for and guiding us in the right direction just saying I love you would have helped a lot. Sure, this is coming from a young pregnant and impressionable teenager, but I had no other perspective to view this from. She should not have locked us away for other people to deal with our problems. Giving up was the easy way out. Dealing with it was the real issue. I was forced to talk to people that I didn't care to talk to. I rebelled against everyone and made sure that they would pay for what they did to me, so I acted out and realized that it wasn't hurting anyone but me. While I was in the hospital I saw and heard so much which makes my story that much more painful. The boy in the next room from me tried to hang himself from his room window. Another girl was trying to take pills, and that's when we had to take our shoe strings out of our shoes and we had everything removed from our rooms but a pencil with no eraser and paper that they provided us for class. All of this

Hurt Used To Live Here

coupled with the many other acts that I had been subjected to should make anyone wonder how I survived. After two weeks there I realized that it was a place for me to vent about what was really going on in my life.

I wasn't outside of the crazy home that long but once I got home it all started all over again. I tried to change for a couple of weeks until I saw that nothing was changing at home. I just went back to my own ways. It wasn't me that needed to change; it was the people that were causing me to go insane that needed to change. I sit here and ask myself all the time, why are you the way you are? Why did I end up with the family I have? Is it a punishment from God to my mom for walking out of the clinic instead of going through the abortion process? I also knew that I wasn't reacting like this for any unknown reason. I prayed not to wake up. Some people prayed for forgiveness, or money, or luck. I prayed that God would end my life in my sleep. Be careful what you wish for because he will give you just that but in a different form. He won't end your life but will make you feel what the end of the road feels like. Mind you, these are thoughts coming from a young teenage girl facing an unwanted pregnancy.

Crying for HELP:

I used to write my mom so many letters about why she treated me the way she did? Why she made me do everything? Writing letters was the only time I felt I could talk to her. I wrote different letters to her about different things all the time. How she used to make me clean my sister's room up when I was 7 months pregnant.

Her room looks like a hoarder's room and it took me all day to do it, but I viewed it as a punishment for me. How I still hated her because she let my dad go scot free for a crime against his child.

I wrote my mom a letter telling her that I would never say anything else to her if she made me go live with my dad after knowing that he raped me. She would always tell me that if you keep acting up you will go live with your dad. It would only get worse from the things she would say to me and the words she would use to describe me as her daughter. One could actually think from reading this that I fault my mother for my life being the way that it is, but on the contrary it is just one of many contributing factors. I had already been put out on the streets numerous times by my mother. Clothes thrown out in the streets, cars ran over them and she locked me out of the house. I wasn't new to this at all. When I would leave my mother would call "T-Boz" a lady police officer that drove around Chicago with my picture in her police car. I was a frequent run away as my mom would put it. I would say I would get put out 75% of the time and ran away 25% of the time. That certainly doesn't paint a whole picture of teenage behavior. I think my mom's job was to make me out to be a bad person because she would tell all her friends and family that I was this and that.

My mom never had anything good to say about her children. It was always yeah right! She always had to make herself look like the great parent. She always complained about us. The real problem was her and not us. We were only reacting to her treatment towards us and the absentness. You could certainly contribute the various men in our mother's life also.

I felt alone and pregnant.

Joyce Reed

Dear Son,

"Son please forgive me for how I felt as a young girl, regarding you. I didn't know what to feel and I was just a kid myself. I was pregnant with you when I was 14 going on 15. I was just a baby myself trying to have and raise one. Please forgive me. Mommy loves you and won't change it for nothing in the world."

Love Mommy

Hurt Used To Live Here

Joyce Reed

New Look:

I then had my handsome son on October 3rd the same day my great granny died. I was in labor for 12 hours and gave birth to a 7 lbs and 12 oz. boy. The same day that I was in labor I was calling and looking for Cocoa trying to tell him that I was in labor and to come to the hospital, but of course he was on 95th street with his guys. He finally called around 3AM in the morning asking can he come to the hospital. I told his ass hell no and hung up on him. Do you think he would try to come anyway? Hell no! It's not like he was there my entire pregnancy anyway.

Cocoa first left when I was 7 months pregnant. He moved to Iowa and tried to make a family out there. When I saw my son I changed my mind about letting my mom take custody. When I first laid my eyes on him I fell in love. He was an angel in my eyes. I knew that he would love me if no one else would. A woman going through her first pregnancy, especially as a young teenage girl, has to bring out a lot of painful and mixed emotions. It is like you are living in two worlds, one in which you are trying to survive and make some sense out of what is about to transpire, and the other about how to provide and make sense of the child that you will be bringing into this world. It certainly didn't help that my mother did not seem to be there for me.

I recall writing a poignant letter to my newborn child stating:

(Page 99)

Of course, there were many conflicting moments coming out of the birth of my son, my mother's role in it, as well as his father Cocoa's ambivalence. My son was a gift from God. He was 22 ½ inches long. He was so light with these dark tiny ears. My mom had those little tiny ears as well. Now don't get me wrong about my venting on my mother in regard to her role with me in my pregnancy. She knew what I was up against as a young teenage mother and my mother wanted the best for me in a seemingly difficult situation.

November 27, 1997 was the first time that Cocoa came to see his son. He brought him 3 pairs of shoes. He came back from Iowa and brought along his girlfriend to my mom's house. While he was visiting his son, he told me that he loved me and the only reason he got me pregnant was because I was so cute and he couldn't resist. Please! I was so disgusted and told him to leave immediately!

Cocoa then went to jail for 8 years for getting caught down in Iowa. He was sentenced to 8 years and no matter what he did and had done to me and our son I was still there for him. I would drive 6 hours every month to take his son to go see him. I was trying to forgive him for what he had done and tried to maintain and keep some sort of a relationship between him and his son. I am sure a lot of young black women have gone through similar situations and circumstances. He was so happy to see us every month. Cocoa promised not to do it again and never to leave us. He called us so many times that my phone bill would be $900.00 a month. I like to think that I did everything that I could to keep that bond between us. I didn't want my son to grow up without a father like I did. I did that until he got out when Marquis was around 3 or 4 years old.

Sacrifice:

I felt that I had to do what I had to do and that was providing for me and my son Marquis when his daddy Cocoa was locked up.

Joyce Reed

Sometimes people can get a bit judgmental about the decisions that a young teenaged mother might make, but when providing for their child hard choices are made. I decided to sell drugs. I was getting a lot of money and recouping after I ran out. I already knew my connects hanging with the guys in the hood. A lot had come from me hanging with the local gang bangers and hood guys in Chicago. Hanging with the guys had me mixed up in a lot of BS too! I am not trying to paint a pretty picture of a difficult time. Sometimes the life that we choose can have rough edges.

On September 13, 1997 that was the day that of my baby shower and all I remember was that I was standing in the doorway trying to get some air from a long day of friends and family, along with gifts and games. It was dark like around 8 or 9PM and as I see this guy walk in the street he pulls out a gun and shoots at me while I was in the door. He missed of course hitting the bricks of the house and the swing on the porch. I ran in the house in fear that they would try to come back. Are they really shooting at me? Did I do something wrong? Or were they after someone else? After a couple of days I went back to my daily routine – the drug business! On my grind, trying to maintain for me and mine. This was something that was normal to me and seen on a daily basis.

Bad Decision:

In 1998 my cousin, my friend, and I decided that we needed something to spice up our lives. Mind you, we were still young teenage girls. We all had our kids around the same time so we just strapped them on our shoulders and went in to Kmart and stole at least $250 worth of goods a piece. Youthful exuberance! They stopped us at the door with our babies before we could even get on the bus. It was so embarrassing and humiliating. We had to walk out in handcuffs with our kids attached to us still and get in a police truck to be taken down to the police station. I was released and nothing was ever put on my record at all because I was just 15. My dad came to the station just to get my son from me, and he told me to get home the best way I could. I was released at 2AM in the morning with just a bus token in Chicago. I was picked up by a curfew officer and told them I lived at the address that my current boyfriend lived and not my mom's house. The police only cared about me being released to an adult. They wouldn't know if they were my real parents or not. They only asked for ID. I stayed with him for two days until my mom was posting pictures of me outside in the neighborhood. I decided to come back home just to let her know I was ok. Perhaps this was the initial reason why my mother expressed her reluctance about me having a child, as well as her putting me in the mental health center. The next time they left me outside late like that, with no regard to my well-being that two days would turn into two months or longer. Again youthful exuberance! How could they leave me out in the streets that late? Was that punishment for me? That's all my mom and dad wanted to do anyway. Even though my "sperm donor" did what he had done to me my mom still allowed him to discipline us.

My mom wanted to have a good reason to take my baby from me anyway. My mom ended up taking him away from me for about three months. She would not tell me where he was and would raise him to hate me. My mother would tell my son that I was a bad mom and that I hated him, and I guess the experience of getting caught at Kmart shoplifting helped prove that point. She indicated that I gave him up and didn't want him. She talked to my son all the time about how bad I was until it was instilled in his head. He started to hate me and I felt it. He wouldn't listen to me at all. My family hated me and thought all these mean things about me. Why?

Change is GOOD! :

My mom finally gave me back my baby after three months. That experience made me open my eyes and I started applying for apartments on my own. I ended up moving into this low income apartment building in Hammond, Indiana and tried to start my life over. I was now dating a new guy and thought he was perfect, until he slept with my friend. My patience was thin and my tolerance was very low. One day my son yelled and screamed for such a long time and wouldn't stop so I whooped him leaving marks on him. I felt so bad and maybe realized to myself that I was not quite ready for all this. I then just dropped him off over to my mother's house because I couldn't deal with all the yelling and screaming and crying. After all, I was just a baby myself! It was driving me crazy. He was then taken from me again but by choice. This time I needed to go back to school and get my GED because I was kicked out during my junior year in high school.

I tried to go back to school but it just wasn't for me and I blamed everything on everyone and never took the time to look at what I was doing to my life. Clearly, and now in retrospect, I didn't have a clue as to what I was doing. I have to live for me and my sons now. I have fashioned my life to be a role model for them. But At that time, I thought how could I do that and I didn't finish school?

I thought at this point I needed to change for my son, and for me. I was now 16 and kicked out of high school. I was working at Popeye's for 2 years until I had to quit. My manager would pay me, even if I didn't work and someone found out. He came to me and asked if I could leave so he wouldn't lose his job. I actually did because I was ready for a new road in life. I enrolled in GED classes and attempted to take the test several times. I would go to my mom's house in such excitement saying mom "look I took the test," and like always I would get a sideways face or glance and a "yeah right." I was used to it. That was my cue to walk away and don't say anything but at that age I didn't let anything slide. I said something to her and before I walked out the door I hear my mother telling my son look at her she leaving you again. I couldn't wait to get my baby back, but I had to be straight first! After the 4th time taking the test I just gave up. I just couldn't get that math together. I put all my faith in GOD to guide me the rest of my life if he was real. I was determined to get a good job. I went to college without having a Ged and I received my associates in accounting and diploma in business.

Afterwards I started at a hospital for 4 years as an accounting clerk until I quit. I then lucked up again and got another job for a hospital call center again no GED or diploma. God was following me and protecting me all the way! I always left that blank when they asked you if you had your high school diploma on the application. I prayed that they would never check. I got through life without it thus far why not keep going. I was at my job at the call center when I got a phone call from someone saying, "Joyce I was looking at your resume and was looking to bring you in for an interview." This turned out to be one of the biggest breaks of my life. I was so excited about that because it sounded like the job that I had been dreaming about, despite my shaky past and youthful exuberance. I went for the interview and as I walked to the address I looked up to check that it was the right building I noticed that I was at the federal building trying to get a job with no diploma. I was going to go anyway just because I was there. It was about an hour long interview after taking a test that I'm not good at all on. I can know all the answers but when it's time to take a test I just go blank. I knew that I failed it.

I went home and prayed and to my surprise I woke up the next day with an appointment to take a drug test. I was offered the position! I was like WOW God you are real! I ended up working in the federal building as a contracted private investigator for the federal government. How cool is that? After GOD blessed me with all that good luck and protection I finally got my GED. I held that job until I had to move to give my boys a better chance at life.

Escaping Chicago:

Chicago was getting horrible! Killings, shootings daily, babies dying, pregnant women getting killed, kidnappings, name it and Chicago had it! The gangs were trying to take my baby to the streets so I knew I had to protect him from all danger. I ended up quitting my very good job and moving 2 weeks later to Georgia not knowing a soul, but with a leap of faith and asking GOD to protect us along the way. I didn't even tell my mother until the last minute that I was moving. I did mention it to her but she would give me that "yeah right face" that I was so used to. I left it at that and continued to plan for our move and didn't tell anyone. I wasn't protected but I was going to make sure that my kids were protected from all things bad. If that was moving 800 miles away, then so be it.

Hurt Used To Live Here

Joyce Reed

SIX

Chapter 6

DON'T JUDGE ME!!

I went through my life not loved or wanted. Some people say that I was weird, cool, funny, fun, giving, passionate, forgiving, a bitch, evil, rude, nice, honest, hurtful, mean, a hoe, slut, tramp, name it and it would seem to fit! I will not say that I have experienced so much in my life that everyone was never to be trusted at all. Experience is really the best teacher and from reading this book I trust that you will see that I have been taught. My guards were always up and trusting was never on my list of things to do. I used to walk around not listening to anyone and doing my own thing. You could be talking to me and looking at me in my face and I would only see your lips move, but hear no words coming out. It's nothing that I am now proud about. It was more like the teacher on Charlie Brown; all you heard was "whomp whomp whomp!" I used to feel like my life was over anyway so why not live like I wanted? I grew up learning everything that I was supposed to learn from my parents, actually on my own. Especially in regards to boys and relationships. I was told that if he talks to you it costs, nothing is free. At least, that was my experience in Chicago. Take, take, take, and it ended up causing me to be raped 7 times. Maybe I do sound like a bitter young woman, but anyone else growing up the way I did would probably feel and express themselves the same way. I rebelled to be the person you now see.

I even went on to have my 2nd baby and 2 years after that I went below everything I felt and believed in. I actually danced (stripping) for the first time, because everyone else was doing it and getting good money. In all honesty, this was a form of prostitution. I did it once and couldn't stand the feeling of a man touching and groping me for his own self-satisfaction. I always seemed to do things that I didn't want to do only to survive or get by, or to even fit in. After I left from dancing, I washed my body for 2 hours, hoping that I would get all the different men's smell off of me. I only danced, not stripped, and that felt so nasty! Other girls stayed and got down how they lived. That should not take much imagination to explain either. At this point I was a mother and knew that still having that feeling of a man on top of you while he does his thing and I'm lying there biting my nails and wondering what I was going to do after or what bills I was going to pay after this fool got off of me! Just hurry up with your business and get off of me. Are you done yet was my favorite question? I realize now what that says about me, or the particular lifestyle that I was living in. That's all I worried about before and after having 2 kids, and I still feel the same way then something needed to be changed and ASAP.

I was tired of being called weird and crazy so I had to prove myself to everyone. I was not a lame nor was I weird at all. They had no clue what happened in my life previous to this. I didn't care to explain either! I was always a loner so losing friends or family was nothing new to me. I had so much hate in my body that it showed in my face all the time. I rarely smiled at all. People used to say "smile girl, why you looking so mean?" They didn't know that if looks could kill, their ass would be dead right then and

Hurt Used To Live Here

there! I would curse anyone that said anything wrong to me or to even look crazy at me. Mind you, this is the product of several rapes, mental and verbal abuse, as well as enduring deaths back to back in my family. I didn't care if it was your mom, dad or your grandma. She had something to say to me, believe me I had words for her too. If you trace this story back to my early childhood, from seeing deaths in the streets of Chicago, you might understand how I could evolve into the woman I am now speaking of. I didn't understand at that time that you need to respect your elders. No matter what it was about me and no one or nothing else. I hated every man that came across my path. I wanted to take from them all. I would always stay ahead of what others did. I kept a wall up. I thought that everyone was after me or trying to take from me. So my guard was always up. I treated men like shit. I ran over them and took all I could from them and faked every minute of it. It now makes me think of how much, if any, I have changed from this behavior. It makes me think of if these previous situations has transformed me into a Dr. Jekyll and Mr. Hyde persona.

    I met this guy in Home Depot parking lot one day going to get a few items and he goes on to introduce himself and asked can he call me. I said sure you can but my phone will be off tomorrow. We had a cool conversation while shopping for my few items. I went on with all my problems that were made up at that time and even cried a tear to a man that didn't know anything about me. That trick worked all the time for me also. When we left the store and he said walk with me to my car I have something for you. I'm thinking to myself. What the hell does this nigga want? I walked to his car in the parking lot and I see a brand new drop top hard top BMW my eyes were like yes I found a good one! He opened his driver's door and reached in and then turned around to hand

Joyce Reed

me $300.00 in cash to pay my phone bill and gave me his number. I certainly can't guarantee that this is how it will work for other young enterprising and opportunistic young women though! I wasn't really surprised that I just came up on a lame. I always had men offer me things and didn't know me. I sure did pay my phone bill and lost his number in the process not on purpose either. Oh well, I'll just move on to the next victim!

I loved my life at this point because I would have all the new cars and motorcycles in front of my house. One would leave and the next one would come. People called me a hoe and slut just because I had it like that and I was using them. I felt that if a man took so much from me –why not return the favor? Out of the men that I ran into, used, played, lied to and didn't care two cents about, I only fell in love with one and really liked two of them. I guess that should give readers some insight into my personality. I knew how to play the role. I cried so many different times just to get what I wanted. I would say my mom is really sick and she is dying or I'm pregnant or I'm about to get put out of my apartment, I just lost my car, whatever you can think of! I lied to a man about it. It paid the bills and I got what I wanted and needed until they weren't useful to me anymore or they started getting clingy. I would tell them all, that my name was Tiffany.

Tiffany was my alter ego she didn't care about shit, not even life! If a guy wanted something I felt that I had to give it to him, because like my mom said, nothing was free.

Only with the men that I did like a little I would have sex to get my hair done to get shoes for my son. Pampers that I needed for my babies I did what I felt I had to do to survive in the streets. Sometimes I felt that I would have to give in. I always felt unloved all the time. What else could possibly go wrong at this point in my life?

Hurt Used To Live Here

Not the 2nd One Too:

I was 19 and pregnant with two different baby daddies nowhere to be found. One of them was in and out of jail since I was 7 months pregnant and the other "sperm" donor just left his responsibility to protect his other life that he had. He ran out on all of his children to be happy after he won a small settlement. He was just living it up, buying buildings and homes, taking trips and living the lavish life while I'm struggling with his son. We (women) have to put our dreams on hold to raise children that didn't ask to be here and it does truly take a mother and a father to raise that child. Deadbeat daddies don't know anything about that at all. How could you? I hope that it all was worth it because you missed so much in his life. There were so many things in my life that I regret doing and saying, but I can't change what I did or said. I can only change from this point on in my life. This Hurt Used To Live Here can be my final epitaph, especially when you take into account all the experiences that I have shared.

Being Verbal:

The things that I write in Hurt Used to Live Here are stories that I learned which have made me the person that I am today. That are things that I am not proud of that I have done things that I have said to people and not even caring about their feelings, thoughts or reactions at the time. If Joyce had something to say she was going to say it! Still now to this day I have finally realized that there is a time and place for everything. We all have to grow and learn in our own time. I used to not care if we were in a store, grandma's house, bus stop, car, restaurant, or even Church, I was going to get my point across and if that took me yelling to the top of my lungs, then so be it. If you had something to say too I was definitely going to put you back in your place. Growing up, I didn't have a voice or opinion, so when I got to that point I wasn't going to take anymore verbal abuse or neglect. I used it with my words. I had words that would make you cry! I'm not proud of that. I just wanted to be finally heard. Verbal abuse was normal to me. I often heard it from family and partners. I used to go from 1 to 10 in 2.3 seconds when it came to verbal abuse. There was no medium with me. It should not be surprising that my life would start to take on a different direction, especially after the birth of my 2nd son and the numerous rapes. Men had not been that accountable to me in my life either.

Strange Moments:

When I gave birth to my second son, when I first laid eyes on him, he reminded me of my brother Michael. As my son grows up he looks more and more like his uncle. It started to get scary when my son was around 4 years old and he would always treat me like I was his woman. It sounds strange but my son would always make sure I was ok. He always made sure if I was tired he would relax me with a shoulder rub or get me something to drink. It may seem normal to some but the way my son looked at me and told me that he loved me was no way a son tells their mom. He would grab my face to face his face and hold my face and say I love you, so passionately. It made me very uncomfortable, was I just over reacting or thinking to hard?

This day he sat down next to me on the couch and put his arm around me and said mommy, how do you feel? I said I'm ok, why? I'm just wondering because you look tired. "Son, mommy is tired but I'll be fine." We began to watch TV and he bust out to say mommy,

"It hurts when you die!"

I said, "What?"

He said, "I said it hurts when you die and when people do bad things they go to hell and GOD don't like those people."

I said, "Yes son, you are right about the bad people, but how do you know that it hurts when you die?"

He said, "Because I just know" and gave me this look like, how else do you think I know.

I was speechless and the only thing I could do was excuse myself and go to the bathroom and cry my eyes out. That's when I really started to believe in reincarnation.

Another time, when I was going through some of my old pictures and around this time, my son was around 3 or 4 and Michael's obituary fell out from my pictures and he said, "Mommy look that's me, that's me."

I said, "No son that's your Uncle Michael."

He said, "I know who that is because I am Michael."

I was so scared of my son because how did he even know who he was at all?

He also used to stand over me while I slept.

You're in Control:

Don't let anyone take you out of our comfort zone or allow you to get that upset to where you have to harm someone or yourself to prove a point. Just count and walk away, as hard as it may be. You can do it! You will be the bigger person by just walking away not giving the other person the reaction they want. You can piss

Joyce Reed

a person off just by not entertaining the situation; they hate when you give them the silent treatment and ignore them. They then realize how stupid they look.

So call me what you want, words are just that, words!! It doesn't make you who you are.

Take it in, let it go in one ear and out the other and keep it moving. People are natural haters and love to hurt people, it always seems like the ones you love or give your trust to always hurt you the most.

Judging me:

I used to let words get to me and make me so angry that I would do things and take it out on the wrong people. I was called a "hoe" all my life because I was pretty. I was called "weird," because I was quiet. I was called "stuck up," because I liked to dress nice. I was called "strange," because I had my own opinion. I was called "skinny," because they were insecure with themselves. I was kicked out on the streets because I opened my mouth and expressed myself. I was disrespected because I let my guards down. I was hurt because I let you get comfortable. I was taken advantage of because I wasn't taught any other way. I was angry because you always pissed me off and tried to run over me. I was abused because it was a normal routine in my life. I let you in because I trusted you and you fucked me over, and now you made a monster. I accepted you because I trusted you. I was the way I was because I was alone. I made mistakes because I raised myself.

I want to thank everyone that had part in making my life the way it has been so far and all the nasty words and the nasty comments and talks behind my back and to my face has made me stronger, more confident, and able to achieve anything that I set my mind too. Thank you for being hateful, mean, and disgusting.

Only one person can judge me and that person is not able to be seen. My father, my GOD!!!

Joyce Reed

SEVEN

Hurt Used To Live Here

Chapter 7

MEN - VS - WOMEN

It all started when I was a little girl, my first non-experience with a girl when I was 8 years old. We didn't know what the hell we were doing. I would ask to look at her breast and when I would see a woman, I would get this feeling that I liked looking at women's bodies but never understood why and how. I was only 8 years old.

A different experience:
What I was doing at 10 years old seemed to come back to haunt me and impact my growth as a woman. I certainly recall that I used to dry hump a female in the middle of the night when I was around 10 years old and we used to even set our alarm clock(s) to meet up in the bathroom to dry hump for around 10 minutes and go back to sleep. That was a very different experience for me but I liked it and you could probably say that was the metamorphosis into the Joyce that is writing this Hurt Used to Live Here novel. I was very curious as I was introduced to it at a young age. Although I knew I was not quite ready for it. That's when I began to like looking at other women's breasts all the time. I know, this is quite a departure from the main thrust of this book, but it certainly has made me who I am now. One might ask where does sex and hurt

fit into this story? This really is my other life. My other first sexual experience with a girl is one in which I learned so much from – good and bad. I finally got the guts to have sex with a woman for real this time without clothes on. She was almost 15 years my senior and I called her freaky Keisha. After dealing with her she made me have a different outlook on women. Keisha should have been called "Keyshawn" as she was more like a grown ass man in a woman's body. She was rough and very dominate. She was rough and we ended up having drunk sex, and the next day I ended up with sore breasts and a sore vagina. I couldn't even put on a bra or wear panties. Yes!! It was horrible I didn't enjoy anything about it! Keisha sucked on me so hard that it was unbearable even to raise my arms to put on deodorant. I was like "hell no" I'm not messing with women if they act like that. "Freaky Keisha" was reckless. Thanks but no thanks. She made me not deal with women for like 6 months, until I meet this pretty light skin girl with no kids who had a banging body with a job and a car. Shhhh! I thought I hit the lotto! You don't find that in a package together and on top of that she was smart and from the "hood." I was like yeah she will change my mind on how I feel about women. I thought to myself; let me give this a try again. I ended up getting up with her mind you this was my first sexual experience with a woman that I took part in it 100%. After she was in the tub getting fresh she walked in the room and lays on the bed. As she opens her legs I am kissing on her neck and chest and moving my way down to finally get a closer look at what a real woman looks like in real life, not being drunk or tackled by a woman or watching it on TV. My hands goes down her leg while I'm rubbing between her thighs. I'm massaging her thighs and work my way up to the "pot of gold." I learned from a man that a smell test is always necessary when dealing with females. I did just that and as I stuck my hand up by my face so I can get a whiff of what I was heading to, it hit my face before my hand did. It was like a smell that I never smelled before. It was a combination of fishy odor with a mildew after shock. It was yet another disappointment for me. She was such a pretty girl! The killer wasn't just that she was foul; the killer was that she just got out of the tub and still smelled! I made up a lie to get out of there. I knew this couldn't be happening to me again. I again took another break form women.

The start of something NEW:

In the summer of 2000 my friends and I decided to walk to the store and as we were walking a car pulls over and it is a car with 3 women in it. They all got out of the car and the cutest one walked up to me. She was so cute, and a different nationality, possibly Korean. She carried herself like a boy, which was somewhat understandable to me because I was a tomboy and wore a lot of boxer shorts because they felt comfortable to me. I hated bras I used to take them off when I got to school. I hated tight clothes on me so I understood why she wanted to wear comfortable clothing. Her name was Abby and she made me feel so good and she knew all the right things to say. She wanted to take me out but I was scared to do that. I was like what will people think about me – is this normal? Is she going to want to hold hands, or kiss in public? I was so scared and always made up excuses. Abby and I kept this going for 2 years. I had to keep this secret from everyone because I was always being judged – so I wanted to make sure that this was what I was really feeling and what I really wanted before I told anyone.

Joyce Reed

Almost:

I got drunk one day and decided that this is the day that I will finally sleep with her. We get to her friend's house, along with other girls, and we talked, played games, and continue to drink even more. Now it's 2am in the morning and it's time to lie down, and as I laid down she began to rub on me and caress my body. It was feeling so good that I didn't want her to stop at all. When she got down to un-bottoming my pants I stopped her and told her that I was ready to go home. I made every excuse that there was such as I'm bleeding, my stomach hurt, etc. I was really scared!

What will she think about me?

Will she look at my stretch marks?

Would she not like me anymore?

Would she be crazy?

Would I go crazy?

So much going through my head all at once all I knew is that I just wanted to go home. She was very understanding and respected my decision and did just that. When I reached my house, I was so happy to get out of that car but upset with myself because I didn't know if she would still want to talk to me after this.

Abby began to write me letters and leave them on my mom's porch at 2:00 and 3:00 in the morning. I got scared and thought that my mom would disown me because she didn't know that I was dealing with women so I told Abby that we could not see each other again. She was sad and hurt but I didn't want anyone to judge me. Of course, in time all of that would change, what I thought of people and their judging of me. I ran from my true feelings or at that time what I thought were my true feelings and what I wanted to do. I knew that a girl didn't make me feel like a man did. I felt like she understood me and didn't want anything from me but friendship and happiness. At this point, I had been raped, fondled, or violated 7 times already and didn't trust a man and when Abby showed me something different that's when I thought that was how I wanted to feel and being with a woman was the only way that I was going to get it. I was ready to try something new and see how this goes.

A couple of months later I came out to the everyone and wrote this letter to my family.

8/23/2001:

Dear Family,

I know everyone is wondering why you all are sitting here. But there is a real good reason for it. Today everything is coming out and no more trying to figure it out. Before I tell you the good and the bad news here is a summary about everyone and how I feel. I then went down the list from Mom, to sister to auntie. As I finished I continued to read on about what had happened to me with my dad and that my mind will never be the same ever again. I feel like my body is no good – how I don't trust ANYBODY and never will. I went on to say that I hate it when they talk to their friends about me or behind my back and it hurts to hear your business in the streets from neighbors and friends. I was begging for guidance and not to be yelled at all the time for every little thing I did. I then blurted it out after reading everyone – I'M BI-SEXUAL everyone!

I was sitting at the head of the table and all I saw were mouths fly open and eyes staring down on me all at once. It was a very awkward moment for me. My sister was the only one that looked at me in disgust and anguish. I just said love me regardless.

I then felt relieved that I didn't have to worry about sneaking around. I was tired of meeting different guys and faking it to my family. I used to have male company just to make my mom happy and out of my business. Half of them I didn't even like or had seen only once or twice. I really had no feelings anymore for men because I was always shown the same thing from them all, especially after what I have experienced with men, I was not interested either. I needed to try something new and different. I used most of them for their money and riding around looking good in their cars. I was always taught that if a man is in your face they need to pay! I did just that and was raped many times for thinking that way.

Ladies, don't ever think that a man is supposed to give you something. Get out and get your own money and be independent." Nothing is free but like that person for what they are worth and not what they have physically. If that man or woman was to stop talking to you then you would be doing this all over again meeting someone and adding numbers to your list. A man thinks that if they are spending money on you, you better be doing something for him. No man or woman will respect you if you don't respect yourself. At the end of the day he's dropping you off to get to the next girl or talking down about you to his homies, or pulling up hollering at the next girl. Ladies, it's still not your car or money, so the question is.

Where is your money?

I finally got that off my chest after realizing that I am into women and really don't know what I was doing with men anyway. It's like when you eat apple pie and try it with ice cream and realize that you can never again eat apple pie without ice cream. I was hooked! I broke up with Abby but was still interested in girls. I was going to see what was out there and see where this girl on girl thing takes me. After all the men I ran into were all the same and they all just let me down.

My first male love:

I meet him when I was 16 or 17 and he was like no other he was smart, cute, and was boyfriend material. I knew he would be different than all the rest I used for money, errands, conversations, and sex talk or used to show off to his friends. I felt different about him. We began to kick it, we went to the show and we rode around a lot. He had a nick name "blues clues" because he wore a suit everyday but this one day it was blue and that's how he got that name from one my friends. It wasn't just about getting in my underwear, he wanted a future with me and we had dreams like buying a building and getting us a house together. We always rode around looking at different property and imagining it was ours. He let me drive his car all the time too. He lived alone so we were free to do whatever we wanted. He was also business minded and I liked that about him. Without saying too much to each other while we was around we knew that love was in the air without even saying a word to each other. I use to spend the night over and when I would awake he was already at work and he made sure he left cab money and a rose every morning for me. He would sometimes leave notes, for me that would make me smile the whole day. He was a gentleman. I met his mom and she was a very nice lady that likes to talk a lot. It was never a dull moment with her either. There was always a new story with her and she wasn't the type to hold her tongue either. I liked that about her,

Joyce Reed

because I was the same way. I knew we would get along great.

This relationship went on until 2000 until he told me that he had another girl pregnant at the same time I was. That just hurt my heart because I got pregnant because that's what he wanted. I was told that I was not leaving and was going to have a baby by him. This was when I was fed up with him and decided to start just dealing with women. When I found that out, that another woman was pregnant the same time I was by the same man. I was a few months and I wanted to get an abortion because it wasn't fair to me that I was lied to and betrayed by the one and only man that I thought was special and was nothing like the rest. All I was thinking was I can't take care of another baby alone.

I stopped communicating with him but he would still try to stay in contact with me to check on the baby and myself. He would ride down on me un-invited or just ride down my mom block to see who was out there. Being nosey! He would sometimes see me talking with guy friends and it would piss him off. The only thing I wanted from him was the money to get an abortion and he said no, basically. His mom was trying to do everything she could and I was trying to scrap every cent I had but it's getting too far along. When I got all the money I needed for the abortion, I called to make my appointment and it went up $300 because I was now 4 months pregnant. This was a sign, not to abort my baby. It had nothing to do with a man, it was out of my control at this point and the only thing I had to worry about was getting ready to have another baby at the age of 19. I couldn't be selfish. It was going to be yet another lonely and sad pregnancy, my un-born child had nothing to do with a no good man. It wasn't as bad as my first son father because his dad was still around but just made really bad choices in life, but this one had to juggle two women that was caring his baby and didn't want her to know but felt it was best for me to know that she was pregnant. I was used to men leaving, so I felt that revenge was needed. I wanted his life to be miserable like mine. I was talked into filing child support from his family. That's not what I wanted; I never wanted to force a man to take care of their responsibilities if they didn't want to. I knew he would pay for it eventually. I was tired of paying people back for the wrong they done to me. I was tired of it honestly. I was exhausted; I let it go until I heard this shit.

When he first laid eyes on him:

When my son was born I was told by his own father that he didn't have his shape of head and his feet weren't his feet. I just gave birth and almost died on the delivery table and the first thing you have to say is he doesn't have your shaped head and feet. He was hours old, he doesn't even have fully shaped nails. I think he was trying to get out of the truth and his responsibilities as a MAN!!! My son was another angel sent from GOD, he gave me hell while in labor too.

His heart rate stop and the doctors made me push at 7cmm instead of giving me an emergency C-section. Mind you, you are supposed to start pushing when you are 10 cmm not 7. I was split from front to back; it took them 2 hours to stitch me up below. I couldn't use the bathroom on my own; I had to carry a big ice pack in my underwear for 2 weeks. I wasn't given any pain medication or anything while I was in the hospital either. I was left in a room alone taking care of a baby and I couldn't even move. They gave me the birth control shot a day after labor, which made me bleed for 4 months straight, non-stop. That hospital messed me up from the time I was there till the time I left. I was already in labor for 4 days and in the hospital due to a migraine that wouldn't go away at all.

You have no idea what I wanted to do to him but instead I did something else to hurt his feelings. When my son was 3 months old, he came over and gave me my monthly allowance as I called it, for the baby and I sat him down and told him that my son wasn't his baby.

The only reason I did that was because he wasn't there 100% and in and out of his life and I was dating someone else that was there for me and my baby. I let him go be with his other family and I wanted nothing to do with him. If you ever want a man to run far away just tell him that you lied about him being the father. He ran so fast that he stop answering my calls and stop calling for a couple of years until my son was 3 years old.

I filed for child support because he was not going to get away with bringing a child in this word and abounding him. My son was struggling from severe nose bleeds that caused him to have low blood and be weak all the time. I was in an out of the hospital every month. My son did not ask to be here. I also felt the need to tell his other baby mama that there was a child the same age as her son and it was by the same man. After being persuaded by his other baby mother and his family. We had a 3 hour conversation about the sperm donor. I was getting questions to the 3rd degree. How, when, what and why? I was happy to answer all of the questions she had for me. Not knowing that for 10 years I would get private calls, threaten text messages all the time. I didn't know that one phone call would lead to this. I had to put an end to all this mess and just get a DNA test that I've been trying to get since my son was 5. I just wanted to prove my point because the message I would get was like: "you fuckin hoe ass bitch that isn't my baby, I'm taking you to court, don't call me anymore," just different rude messages. I was glad to put this to an end. I know I told him that, my son wasn't his but after a couple of years passed I reached out to him telling him that I would pay for the DNA test to prove that he was his son and that I lied. I would take full responsibility and pay for it myself. Still nothing!

After all the phone calls, text messages, private calls ,taking the DNA after 9 years of my son life it came back 99.9999% you are the father. "in my Murray voice" I thought this would end the phone calls but NOOOOO I'm still getting calls from his wife now but girlfriend then about her not believing the test and to send her the papers. I laughed in her face and said get it from your husband! Hung up right in her face. Phone calls didn't stop until I just decided to be a woman about the issue and realized that this was bigger than us; it had everything to do with the kids. It started out good when we were able to be on the phone and be civil with each other until I let my boyish ways and flirtiness get involved; now the tables were turned.

Oooo and you cute too!!

My Break:

At this point I wanted to stop dealing with men and just deal with women. I would be sexless because the women that I was running into were rough or wacky as hell in bed. I said fuck it, I'll just be bi-sexual but only deal with one or the other. Let's not lose fact of the matter that I was also the mother of two sons.

Ladies if you are bi-sexual please don't deal with both sexual partners at the same time. You can tell the difference when a woman is sleeping with a man – meaning if you are sleeping with a man and decided that sleeping with a woman is a good idea in the same week. That's a "no no" there are so many STD's out here that you can get from a man or a woman. Only deal with one class of sexual partners at a time and always use protection. Just think about who that girl has slept with, then who that man is sleeping with. The list goes on and on both sides.

Starting Over:

In 2001 I tried this thing again – I meet a wonderful girl. This is when they had gay nights in Chicago on King Drive. I was introduced to her by another gay guy friend. She was so cute and nice. She was also a "stud" someone that dresses more comfortable in men's clothing and sometimes having a mindset of a man or their swagger is somewhat of a man, but looked like a girl. We begin to talk and date. She was so sweet to my boys and loved Martrel to death – she spoiled him like crazy. After meeting her she taught me that there are good people out here and it wasn't just about sex either. We were together for two years and never had sex. For other reasons that I respected and vice versa. I was bisexual she didn't like that. I respected that and left all men alone for her after a while. A girl had needs even though they never got fulfilled anyway because the men I was dating or dating thus far was not hitting on shit. I faked it so much with the men that I even got my leg shake together.

My boyfriend at that time was not having that at all. He was cheating on me anyway so my feelings were not there anymore. He knew that women were my main interest anyway. I started playing him to the left and not returning his phone calls. He started showing up at gay club scenes where I would party at, or showing up at my house unannounced. I didn't want to continue hurting his feelings so I told him I was serious about dealing with women. It was a turbulent period for me and my boys. There was untold hurt for me and my family, which is what this book is about, but it is also about closure. I can't help but wonder what my life would have been about if not for that painful and unfortunate rape of me by my father, or my mother not believing me at the time and supporting me. I have to be a bigger person for my sons and not get blinded by what happened to me. Sure, Hurt Used to Live Here, but I can honestly say that I am moving ahead despite it, and I want to make a life for my sons that they will be proud of.

Joyce Reed

EIGHT

Chapter 8

LOVES ALL - TRUST FEW!!!

It's easy for some people to say I LOVE YOU; some people use that word loosely and use it all for the wrong reasons. I was one of those people. I would tell you that I loved you and cared about you and most of the time I didn't mean it.

I never would tell someone first that I loved them because I knew that 9 times out of 10 I really didn't mean it or wasn't ready to say it. I didn't want karma to come back on me so I just waited for them to say I LOVE YOU and I would say; dang my other line, or "what you say," or "I do too" or "me too."

When you first meet someone, they are the nicest and sweetest people ever. They open the door for you, send an "I'm thinking about you" text, send you flowers, and surprise you with your favorite things. Until they get comfortable and they change like that. Is that love or lust of is it just being controlling? They always tell you what you want to hear like:

I love you like no other.
I will never hurt you.
I will never cheat on you.
You are my first.
I can't live without you.

What will I do without you in my life?

I accept you, flaws and ALL.

They say all the things you want to hear until it's time to put those words into action. We all know that actions speak louder than words. Along with the lies and betrayal, why can't you just keep it real and be a real man or real woman and be upfront and honest with your shit?

Instead I get letters like this:

Joyce Reed

"When I look at you I see everything I want to see. You're pretty brown eyes, your soft skin and your pretty face. I wonder sometimes if any woman can take your place. It will be hard though because when I look at you, I see everything I want to see. You're everything I want you to be. You make me weak every time I touch you.

Signed, I lied!!

Hurt Used To Live Here

Joyce Reed

I always said that a person can never trust you if they don't trust themselves first.

I have only been in love two times in my life and one was with a man and the other 1 was a woman I was really in love with, and not just lusting over them or loving there sex…When I say I was in love with them I mean that, I really cared, cherished and trusted them in every way. We had a friendship before anything and I would be hurt if that was ever taken from me. No matter how long it's been, you always know your first love and your true love. You know who you are when I say that I loved you more than I loved myself, I loved your friendship, your honesty, intelligent words, companionship, trust, love making, I loved your flaws and all, I loved the way you held me, grabbed me, looked at me, touched me, being in a crowded room but only seeing your face, I loved everything you had to offer. You know who you are and you were my first true love. You gave me something on a different level and I would not change it for anything in the world.

Even though you hurt me again and again, I know that it wasn't intentionally done, most of it was out of our control and in due time we will reunite again like we always do and they say 3rd time's a charm… You said to me that when you leave me it feels like you are leaving your heart and when you leave her it feels like you leaving the kids... I will always remember that.

Even after my life has proved to me that everyone was out to get me, I never thought that I would find someone like you to love me for me and you never judged me.

When we met again it was like the first time we laid eyes on each other and those same butterflies where still flying in my tummy. It has been this long and we still share the same feelings. Thank you for being you.

Karma:
   I think all the things I did to people in the past years when I was angry was coming back to get me. I know I have told some lies to get what I wanted but I thought that's what I was supposed to do because of all the bad things that happened to me. I was out to hurt anyone that came across my path and didn't care. When it was time for me to really love, it back fired on me and I was left alone and hurt. After noticing that I never had a relationship over 3 years was like a routine for me that I needed to change a few things and fast. I used to find every little thing that would be wrong with someone to break up with them. Like they chew ugly, I hate the way they walk, why did they just say that? I'm bored as hell with you, time to move on. It was easy to break up and move on because I was always one step ahead and always kept a backup plan. I made sure that I will never be lonely again.
   It was only a hand full of people that I did trust and I didn't trust them as far as I could throw they ass. The ones I could trust were my true friends that stuck by me no matter what.

WTF:
   Who are you to look down on me and tell me who you think I am, who the fuck do you think you are?
   You come to me and whisper sweet nothings in my ear and tell me how much you care about me. Make me feel good and caress my body all night.
   Who are you to do all these things and change overnight?
   Why did you betray me?

Why did you tell everyone the secret I told you last night?
Why did I give you my trust and you stomp on it?
How could you do that to me?
Why are you smiling and thinking that hurting me is fun and games to you?
Is this enjoyable to you?
Are you getting a kick out of this?
How could you do this to me after I gave you all of me?
I gave you all of me and in return you gave me heart ache and pain.
Noooo, baby come here, I didn't mean that. I didn't mean to have sex with her. I was hurt from the neglect. I wasn't thinking or was I drunk? You know I love you and would never do anything to hurt you again. Baby, these tears are real. Here baby, I went to the mall today and thought about you. Baby take me back. I'm soooo SORRY!!
How could you believe them?
They are lying on me. You know I wouldn't do anything like that. I love you baby. Please baby please!!
How could someone be so cold to you?
It made no sense to me at all. The things people would do to get out of trouble.

Hurt Used To Live Here

Joyce Reed

NINE

Chapter 9

FRIENDS & HATERS

People go around calling everyone their friend. I learned the hard way that everyone is not your friend. Some people are in your life for a reason or a season. Some good, some bad, some just plain old nosey and just want to be in your business. Well, I have had all of the above and more. It was always hard for me to trust people, let alone a woman because the most important ones have betrayed me. For example, I knew a girl that wanted everything that I had, she slept with 5 different people that I dated, had a child by, or was in love with or even spoke to. It was like she wanted to have everything that I had but then again she slept with all of her friend's and sister's men too. Like really is it that serious to have what I have or had!

There was another girl that I don't even care to mention by name that also wanted to be me. She stole my style, my money, the bitch even tried to steal me! No one really cared for her at all. She never smiled and hated anything that I loved. She always made herself available for everything that she wasn't invited to. She ate everything that wasn't pinned down. It got to the point of being overwhelming when she tried to fit in where she was never wanted and just didn't belong. She tried to ruin a longtime friendship, and actually did. She always wanted everyone to themselves, her friends never having any friends outside of her.

Joyce Reed

She is a very jealous person – when we all saw that she was trying to break the crew up we just started kicking it all together and leaving her out. It was always about her and what she thought and what she did and what she knows. She would literally make my ASS HURT!!! It was ridiculous for a grown ass woman to be acting in this manner. Our fake ass relationship lasted 3 years too long! She a fake, phony, miserable ass bitch! You know exactly who you are.

Real Friends:

There are also some great friends that I still have to this day. They have been there for me through good and bad and my ups and downs – never once judged me or talk about me behind my back. They have been an inspiration to me in my life in some shape, form or fashion.

I've been called some nasty names like; weirdo, strange, crazy, sicken, different and whatever else you can think of. I say to myself that you are the one because I AM different and don't act like everyone else!

I only had a few that I called my real friends and they actually lasted still to this day. Like a really great friend, we have been friends since the 4th grade and we did so many things together and it was kind of hard for her to understand me but she never judged me or never stops being my friend. Even when we were at my mom house on day and my dad stopped by and I hid in the bathroom until he left and she was so confused to why I was hiding and I had to eventually tell her, but I said he raped me and I left it at that. She accepted that and never questions me further; she accepted that I didn't want to talk about it again.

Hurt Used To Live Here

It used to be funny when I told her that I was with my friend.... She would be like, WHO? I've been your friend since 4th grade

Why I don't know them ...?

She was funny and talks really fast, my mom use to say she sound like that girl off the show seven. Sometimes I could keep up but I learned to live with it. I loved her just the way she was and still is.

We used to have fun times and talk about any and everything. She made sure she had the latest everything and did what she had to do to get it. She was a slick talker. She was one of my friends that I knew would never have children but has a handsome son and happily married. I am so happy for her and wish her the best in everything she does.

There is another great friend that I can truly call a friend. I knew her since she was 7 years old. She lived right behind me on May Street. We use to have so much fun because her dad and my step dad would always be in his garage doing something so we always had fun. If I wasn't at her house, she was at my house.

Oh, there was a time when we used to sneak cigarettes out of her fridge and smoke them. I wondered why her mom kept cigarettes in the fridge anyway. We were curious so we tried them and almost choked to death. She used to make the best eggs known to mankind and spiced it up with some hot sauce to give it that spicy breakfast tang. Just what you need early in the morning. . I would come over every morning just to have those famous eggs. She was there for me through good and bad times. She was also my brother's girlfriend. She was in love with him. She was and still is a loving friend and a calm friend; she is always smiling and friendly and a loving mom to her two beautiful girls. Who wouldn't love her? She is my ride or die chick that I know I can count on for anything.

Another friend we have been friends since the 7th grade and it seemed like we shared a lot through the years. We were really close when she had a boyfriend and I had a boyfriend, and they were best friends. We did that twice and It was actually fun. We would all walk home together as couples, get chased by dogs or chased by them all the way to Ada Street, we always had a great time. I would walk to pick her up for school and we walked together every day with our black and gold colors on. Her family was so fun, loving and very funny. She was another friend that I NEVER had to worry about and still the original one bestie.

Friend, even though we grew up on the same block and didn't become close until we were teenagers I can't forget my honey bunches of oats. You have impacted me in so many ways. You never took sides when it came to listening to both sides. You were always the calm friend that believed in real friendship and positivity. If it wasn't perfect then it didn't have your name attached to it. Your passion has been cooking and she made sure when she did cook, she put her foot, arms and legs in it. From her Tilapia, to baked chicken, to her corn beef sandwiches, cat fish filet, sweet potato pie and basically anything that she has cooked was great and will have you coming back for more. Her dream finally came true and she now has the #1 restaurant. The Ultimate Catering Company is an ultimate must have. You have impacted my life in so many ways. Even if you think you didn't, you did. GOD put us together for a reason and not a season it was for a lifetime. I wouldn't trade your friendship for anything in the world, well maybe for red velvet... Joking! I love you.

Friends are so important to me, it's always good to have someone that you can count on and have in your corner when you need them.

Negative Friends:

I do have people that crossed my path and I regret even putting in my life and you know who you are. These are the friends that tried to be your friends for the wrong reasons. Some of them tried to be like me, dressing like me, used me and talk bad behind my back and smile in my face. Fake is the perfect word for them. I had a friend that almost put me in jail. I had a friend that had sex my man, I had a friend that had sex my woman and I had friends that lied on me, or lied to me. That's why they no longer exist in my life.

People use the word friend lousy like they use the word love loosely... A friend is someone that you can have around you man / woman, a friend won't betray you, lie to you, talk behind your back, hang out with your exes, buy a dog because you have one and they know they have bad allergies, or criticize everything you do. If someone's conversation is always about another person or people's drama, best believe that person is talking shit about you too to the next person / friend. Why can't people just mind their own business? If everyone did just that this world would be better off. If a friend seems to always have you down and never move or are able to move forward in life. Some people just have bad sprits. So many great things have happened in my life since I stop fucking with you. Thanks for being a messed up person.

An enemy:

If I ever called you a friend it's because I put enough trust in you to trust you. If you screwed me once, I forgave you but if you do it a second time then it's my time to screw you, only my screw will feel like I bent you over and rammed you with no oil. My motto growing up was you hurt me I make you cry, you make me cry, I make your life miserable. Especially if you did it intentionally. I can go on and on about the way people are and why they do what they do, but it would always be a question and to get the answer to that question is like teaching someone to right with no hands. You would hurt yourself trying to figure it out, just leave those people in your back row. You deal with people like that according.

How can you live your life and you living mines??

Hurt Used To Live Here

Joyce Reed

TEN

Chapter 10

LIES & BETRAYAL

Why do people have to lie so much? Does it hurt to tell the truth? Is telling the truth going to kill you and send you straight to hell?

When I say that some people lie for no reason, it would be somewhat of an understatement. Like; "Yeah Boo! I'm going to pay your phone bill tomorrow," and when tomorrow comes they are nowhere to be found. Cool, you didn't pay my phone bill that is still going to get paid but it is the lie that pisses me off! Not so much the initial lie, but the additional lies added to the first lie... Then you are quick to keep adding more and more lies. "Baby, I woke up in the middle of the night and thought about you and called you to tell you how much I love you..." The next day I hear that you just got back from the club.

If you need to cheat then leave the relationship, because hurting someone's feelings is not a great feeling at all. Doing the hurt or getting hurt, both are hurtful and if you are the giver Karma will be meeting up with you soon. It took one relationship to have all my Karma come back and hit me so hard that I didn't know if I was coming or going. Karma waits until you are happy and think that you are the most comfortable and taps you on the shoulder... Hey buddy, remember me?

The Twist:

I went from being quiet and shy to being blunt and too honest, as they say. I was tired of seeing the same reaction, so I decided to change it up and give honesty. I didn't believe in wasting time, especially my time because I could do something more productive. I had this thing that when or if we had sex or your head game was "whack," I was the one that didn't spare your feelings. I would tap you on the shoulder with my long index finger and look at you in your eyes and say, PLEASE!!!

What are you doing? Please stop!!!

Did I care about hurting their feelings? Hell Naw! There were a few people that got that tap on the shoulders. I felt that they didn't care about wasting my time so why should I? I was very upfront with a lot, like what type of person I was and what to expect from me. If I was looking for a relationship, then you knew that. If I was looking for a winter buddy, you knew just that also. Whatever my intentions, you knew them up front. Even if I wanted a friend with benefits, you knew that.

Betrayal:

There is also this thing where people like to talk behind your back and when it's brought to them they want to lie or deny everything. Now if I smack the shit out of you for having wasted my breath and my time, I would be wrong, right?

I'm not saying that I never lied and I'm this perfect angel because I'm not, This is me growing up and experiencing all the lies I have told has gotten me nowhere but bad luck and bad experiences happened to me. Every experience is a learning experience, good or bad. You don't have to be anyone but yourself. If someone don't like you then you have to understand that they weren't the first and they won't be the last to say they don't like me. I'm not living for you or trying to be someone I'm not.

Betrayal hurts the most when it's from someone you love or very close to. I was betrayed by friends and rumors spread that I was a "hoe", I slept with Jimmy, Terrence and Sarah. I was accused of sleeping with friend's boyfriends, baby daddies, having several sex partners in a day. I was called slut, tramp, and a hood rat. I used to care when I wasn't even having sex and was called those names. As I got older I always wondered why everyone was always in someone else business and not concerned about their own. I think the world would be a better place if they just mind they OWN business. Check YO SHIT first...

Why are you so concerned what Joyce do with her PUSSY?

Do you maintain warmth and confront from Victoria Secrets? Do you provide pants to cover my PUSSY?

Do you provide gas money every year when I have to go for a yearly checkup?

Can't forget maintaining my hard wood floors.... If you can answer YES to ALL then we might me getting somewhere but until then MIND YOUR BUSINESS!

Everything that I was accused of was done to me by family members and friends. A family member slept with my boyfriend at the time, my baby daddy and a guy I was dating. One of my exes slept with someone I knew to get back at me, bitch you the nasty one, you not hurting me. LOL! Some of my family members were sneaky with it but they always got caught. Then they would try to be their friends after we broke up, what type of shit is that?

Joyce Reed

If I'm not with that person anymore, does that give you any right to be friends with them and you didn't even know them? Wacky ass family and friends. Can't forget one of my exes that I really cared about told me that she fucked someone that I really cared about and that she was sorry but she really liked her a lot. This is the BS that I have been thrown from my family and close friends. It takes a lot for me to trust you and if you betray me then shame on you.

As I read my journal in 2002, I was very angry and stayed pissed at people. This is when the men I was dealing with made my transition very easy to women. Men always proved me right all the time. I felt I was missing 85% of happiness from a man. It was always a cheating issue or lies. A woman gave me that same 85% but I realized after 10 years I was still missing that 15%. I needed to find that 100%.

This was sent to me and I want to share it with you......

I am not the owner of the content written below:

Everyone can't be in your FRONT ROW!!!

Life is a theater so invite your audiences carefully. Not everyone is holy enough and healthy enough to have a FRONT ROW seat in our lives.

There are some people in your life that need to love from a distance. It's amazing what you can accomplish when you let go, or at least minimize your time with draining, negative, incompatible, not-going-anywhere relationships, friendships, fellowships and family!

Everyone can't be in your FRONT ROW!!!

Observe the relationships around you. Pay attention to: Which ones lift and which ones lean? Which ones discourage? Which ones are on a path of growth uphill and which ones are just going downhill? When you leave certain people, do you feel better or feel worse? Which ones always have a drama or don't really

understand, know and appreciate you and the gift that lies within you?
   Everyone can't be in your FRONT ROW!!!
   The more you seek God and the things of God, the more you seek quality, the more you seek not just the hand of God but the face of God, the more you seek things honorable, the more you seek growth, peace of mind, love and truth around you, the easier it will become for you to decide who gets to sit in the FROT ROW and who should be moved to the balcony of your life.
   Everyone can't be in your FRONT ROW!!!
   You cannot change the people around you... but you can change the people you are around! Ask God for wisdom and discernment and choose wisely the people who sit in the FRONT ROW of your life. Remember that FRONT ROW seats are for special and deserving people and those who sit in your FRONT ROW should be chosen carefully. Everyone can't be in your FRONT ROW.
   "Un-Known Author"

Those words couldn't be spoken any clearer. People come in your life for a reason and a season. Don't get upset when people talk down about you and judge you. Just know that they will always be in your back ROW and only the real survive.

Joyce Reed

ELEVEN

Chapter 11

MY OTHER LIFE

OMG this new girl was a hand full to everyone. I knew her from high school and we had some of the same friends too. This was my 2nd girlfriend and after dealing with her I was a new person, was it because she made me have my first orgasm EVER… YES first!!! Not from a man EVER but at this point I was in love but didn't know that I would pay for the best orgasm I ever had in life. We ended up being together for 3 years and regretting mostly everything.

Let me start from when we used to fight. I don't think we had many good times, if we did they ended bad. Women are emotional creatures, but she was very different. I mean she was crazy as hell!!! She would go see psychics and come home and fight me about what was the truth and what she believed. She was having dreams about dead people and waking me up with scratch marks on my body, having black eyes, being disrespected, disrespecting my mother, her mother, lies, betrayal, and abuse. She abused night time pills and medication. She thought that was the only way she could sleep at night. She would wake up 3 am in the morning and if she didn't fall back to sleep then she would go to the gas station and grab a pack of tynoyol night-time. She smoked cigarettes heavily. I told her to stop and we both agreed that if she smoked then I was able to hit her in her mouth, every time she thought about smoking. I would hit her so hard that her lip would bleed. I hated cigarette smoke and didn't like the way it smell at all. It was like it was coming out of her pores. She had been smoking for over 6 years. Like a pack a day chain smoker. She stopped for like a couple of days but was back at it. After a while we began to live together, we stayed at her mom's house as well as my mom's house too and it only got worse for us. I started to cheat on her because I wasn't happy and all we knew was fighting and arguing daily. She would break any code I had on my phone, she would hide in bushes and under porches trying to catch me up. She would be friends with my friends to find out anything that was going on. She found out that I met this other girl and she went to my friend's house and tore her entire house up. I wasn't at home at the time so she decided to take her anger out on our friend's house. I told her to leave so she moved in next door to my mom's house just to keep an eye on me. I was so in love that it was hard for me to leave; we ended up having a fake marriage and exchanged rings. It was cute, my friend married us and we did it in the middle of the street. We even had a bachelorette party.

I knew I was in an abusive relationship and I knew it wasn't healthy but I felt that no one else would want me and it was a point where I was scared to leave because I didn't know what she would do to me or herself.

We had a really bad fight and I was tired of her disrespecting me all the time so this last time was very hurtful. I had just had my knee surgery and she came over to accuse me of doing something when I was on bed rest and couldn't even walk let alone deal with someone. I had a tube coming from my knee and was on crutches so me cheating was not on my list of things to do. She came over my mom's house to argue and fight and after arguing after 10 minutes she ran and jump down on my knee that I just had surgery on and I screamed in pain. She tried to run but I jumped up so fast and took one of my crutches and beat her across the head and body with it. She eventually got away and ends up calling a girl to pick her up from my mother's house. I couldn't do anything about it but cry about it. I couldn't move and she knew exactly what she was doing.

I thought this would be our last time around and last fight but I guess that wasn't enough for me. She ends up sneaking into my mother's house after my mother left for work. She left the back door unlocked so she can come back in the house after my mother left for her night shift. This night I went out to a club with some friends and I came home around like 3am and when I walked in the house I notice that it was pitch black and my mom never leaves all the lights off so I felt it to be very strange. I walked through the living room to cut on the dining room light and as I turn on the light I hear a noise from my mother's room and the door slowly opens. I see her coming out from a dark room with a hammer in her hand. I begin to laugh at her and asking her

What the hell are you doing?

She swung that hammer at my face and I knew she was serious and was trying to hurt me. I then took the hammer from her and we fought for a long time. At this time we used to wear those name plated belts, so I took it off and beat her over the head with it. We both were bloody and still fighting.

She was a face person, she was jealous of my eyes so she would always try to poke them out with her thumbs or mess my face up. Come to find out, I wasn't the first person to get a restraining order against her. She was like a nut case that needed a strait jacket. One minute, "I love you boo," and then she cursing you out at the top of her lungs in the same breath. I know that she was a good person at heart and very sweet sometimes. That's why I fell in love with her, but when she mad she mad and everyone will know.

I end up calling the police on her and when the police came my face was really bloody and I had 2 black eyes so the police end up taking her to jail. She stayed the night in jail and we had to go to court and instead of my pressing charges I just told them that she needs help. They gave her 3-4 years' probation and therapy.

That girl was a dangerous one but I know how to deal with her so it doesn't bother me anymore. Just hang up on her ass and don't call her for months, LOL!

I eventually moved on and found happiness with someone else.

Dealing with women:

I was dating this girl off and on and I thought was different from my last relationship and at the time and we had got into an argument earlier that day and we show each other in a club and as I was doing my routine walk around the club. I noticed that another girl was sitting on her lap and as I walked pass and got half way on the dance floor, my body stop in my tracks and turned around. As I turned around I ran up on the both of them and my ex girl threw the girl that was on her lap off her and I swung on my girl with my entire mite and knock her clean off the couch her ass was sitting on. We then proceeded to fight and I was swinging and hitting her all in her head. We get closer to the stairs and all I see is a vision that I kicked her down those stairs. Before I could lift my leg to kick her, she picks me up by my legs to stop me. We end up getting kicked out of the club and took it outside. She pulled up wanting some more. I jump out of my friends' car and attacked her but she start running around the car so I jumped in the car and just started to throw everything out in a puddle of water. Her hat, glasses, cd's, money anything that was in her console or lying around in arms reached was in the water. That's just one of my UN forgettable anger moments.

Just like the rest:

There was another time when my ex use to hit me and verbally and physically abuse me until I was feed up and took her ass to a hotel and had it all planned out. I had strawberries, apples and oranges her favorite. I played like everything was cool and romancing her and even went to the extent of dressing up for her. I tied her up and as I was kissing on her body, I got on top of her and just start thinking about all my black eyes I had to hide from friends and family. Marked up body from the abuse. I beat her face up so bad and continued until I felt I was satisfied. I left her there for an hour or so to think about all she had done to me over the past 3 years and came back in to let her loose and left her there to find her own way home. Of course it didn't stop her at all. She became crazier. She began to hide in bushes and hide under my neighbor's porches.

The END:

On this day it was the straw that broke that camel's back. I let her back in and this night was crazy. We were sleep and I woke up to a punch in my face. I held her and told her that it was a dream and it wasn't true. I knew then how to deal with her and her dreams that she thought were true. She yelled, "you are cheating on me and I know with whom, your grandma just told me." Mind you my granny died in "96" she was crying and screaming that I didn't like her anymore and she would kill herself if I left. This wasn't the first time she attempted suicide in front of me. At this point I was fed up with all of it, this was the last straw for me. I said well if you want to kill yourself then go ahead and do it. She went to the kitchen and grab a parrot knife and held the knife across her neck and stared to cut. I said well I don't see any blood you just want attention, you not going to do anything.. Prove me wrong!!!! I was absolutely fed up! She went to take the knife to her wrist and went across. I informed her that it was the wrong way, yeah I was a BITCH but only judge if you have been in my shoes. She began to go deeper; I then saw blood everywhere and then took the knife from her. She told me that demons were out to get her and she needed me. Yes I stayed and endured more and more abuse from her. My mother kicked us out because I decided to stay with her. We then got our apartment in Indiana and she abused me even more.

We would then find out that we were not good for each other. It took her attacking me with a hammer after breaking into my mom's house. I told her that if we loved each other then we would not continue to hurt each other and continue this bad relationship. I was devastated and hurt for a long time. I didn't get into another relationship for a couple of years again.

I had friends that I would vent to because I was scared of what people would think of me, the gay community was very small and everyone knew everyone. Nothing was private! It took almost 3 months to get rid of all the bruises and scratches I had on my body from her. At the end of it, I was the bad person, she told people that I would beat her for no reason and I was very abusive. Which was a lie, but I'm here to tell the truth. I was only defending myself from what I thought was real love.

After dealing with sicko, I was heartless and was emotionally messed up. I would say to myself, I can't be with a man but I can't be with a girl. I started to use woman and treat them like shit. I didn't understand how men did it but I do sure have a better understanding to why!! Some woman just like drama.

Party Time:

A friend and I were just getting out of a relationship together, so we were determined that we were going to get a new girlfriend or a dip or just something to do until someone came into our life that is worth our love.. My friend used to call me scary all the time. I was scared to approach woman or say anything to them. Sickos made me feel so insecure and ugly. I told my friend that if I get turned down I'm going to go HAM on someone. I hate rejection!

I am known for being blunt and honest. If you don't want the truth then don't ask me. I used to say things to people and don't think about the outcome or what I was saying until after the fact. Saying sorry was not in my vocabulary at all, it literally hurt to say "I was sorry" I wasn't a sorry person, so why say something I'm not?

We started to go to different gay clubs but the most popular was the Generator. That was the spot to get anyone you wanted. Tall, short, skinny, fat, ugly, fine, beautiful, left over's, hoes, bust downs, bums, low life, cheaters, liars, fakers, frontiers, even the wealthy. 2005 was my year that I was not going to ever be alone again.

We started drinking tang and roses lime and anyone that drinks know that tang brings the worst out in you. It did just that! I would start approaching woman without a care in the world. They would always reply with a yeahhh, or what's up. I was then excited about the outcome. More and more drinks made me get out of my body.

These were some of my tang pickup lines:
Oooo, you so pretty.
Heyyyy lil mama.
Where did you get that shirt from "as I am rubbing her arm and looking at her in her eyes?
I know you from somewhere, what school did you go to?
You ass looks nice, can I touch it?

I loved every minute of it, as everyone told me YES. I would meet different women along the way. Interesting women, crazy women, stalker women, nice women, beautiful women, ok looking women, attached women, feminine women, manly looking women, woman trying to be men, married women, dingy women, insecure women even confused woman. I hurt some along the way and I also got hurt a few times. They say KARMA IS A BITCH!!! Yeah I met her a few times. It was about me and feelings weren't acknowledge. If you hurt me, I made sure you hurt 12x's worst.

Very Strange:
I had this one ex and her parents were crazy. She was of age.

She was actually in college at the time and we used to email each other every day and live chat. It was hard for us to see each other because her parents were against her being gay. She was a soft stud, which is "a girl that dresses versatile, both ways." After dating on and off for 2 years, she finally spent the night, not just the night but the weekend. I was a little skeptical but just happy that she was there. Saturday morning approaches and it's time for me to go to physical therapy for my herniated disk I had in my lower back. While I was there, Caquetá decided to cook breakfast for us at home. In the middle of therapy, my mom calls me and tells me that the sheriffs are at her house looking for their daughter and I kidnapped her. WTF! I said, my mom whispered to me, don't go home, they on their way there now. I hung up the phone and called my girl quickly. Yelling get out now, get out of my house. Stop whatever you doing and leave. Your dad is at my mom's house and on their way to my house where you are. She left the house and left my front door open, I was cool with that because I just wanted her to leave. I already left therapy to head that way anyway. My phone rings and I quickly answer the phone thinking it was her and it was her dad. "Joyce we are at your mom's house and I know you have my daughter!" Silence on my end. He said "You might as well come, turn yourself in at your moms' house because we have all of your computer records and emails you all sent back and forward." I was scared shitless and was shaking. After thinking for over an hour, I decided to go to my mom house and just get it over with. I know I didn't do anything, and she was in college so I know she was of age. When I walked in the house there were like 6 police officers and 2 sheriffs. REALLY? ALL this for a girl that wasn't a minor. He questioned me about her and denied everything and didn't give him anything. He was pissed that I wouldn't give him any details. He tapped my computer and my room phone. After they left I was then worried about her and where she had gone. She cut her phone off and I didn't hear from her in over a month. She finally emailed me and told me that her dad took her car and moved her to Mississippi. She was not allowed to speak to me again. She emailed me like 4 years later to tell me that she was still dealing with women and she was dating a girl there. I was happy for her and happy that she finally got away from her crazy parents.

Special:

Let me tell you about Mute. I had a girl that I dealt with since 2004 and she was the kind of girl you would reach out to if you wanted to text all day and night. A lot of goodies that I still get to this day. She would never pick up the phone and talk. She would text all kinds of things. She would text you while we in the same room. We dated and finally became a couple in 2008, it just didn't work out with us but we will always be text buddies. There is never a dull moment with you in my life. Thanks mute.

Messy:

This one made me look sideways about women. She was a girl by day and a stud by night I should have left her alone then. If she lied to her mom about who she really was then why would she care about me? She would literally change her clothes in the car after going out on date with me. It was sometimes funny because her mom had cameras surrounding her house. She couldn't have girl company and her mom was against gay relationships. This waste of time lasted 2 years until I got tired of the games and lies and left. She tried to do whatever she could to prevent me from being happy after her. When I finally took some time to get over her, she still continued to play games until I finally moved on with my life. Then she decided to stalk my home, leave letters and cards in my hallway, call me and text me begging for me back and say she was sorry for all that she did to me. I wasn't falling for it, I and Mute started something together and I was over her games. I eventually had to get a restraining order against her too because she started to email me at work and send threatening messages. She finally moved on with her life until she found out who I was with after me and mute decided to go our separate ways.

You're LOST:

I can tell you this, everyone that I have been with and they know they lied, cheated, and played me have begged for me to get back with them or marry them. Still to this day.

My Motto is: I never go backwards; I left you for a reason.

I have been proposed to 4 times in my life and 2 women have had my name tattooed on them. I must have done something right. No matter what an ex has to say about me, I gave my all in every serious relationship I was in and I'm not about to bash you but I want you to know that your hateful words were the devils words and I forgive you for all you have done to me and against me.

My TRUTH:

I met my Sexy mama in 2005-06. We were just friends; we would share stories with each other. We both were in relationships but weren't trying to pursue each other. I didn't look at her like that; I looked at her as a friend and nothing more than that. We would go out just to hang out with friends and just have fun." In the gay world you are not allowed to have other gay friends especially if they were studs and you were a femme. We would talk every blue moon just to check on each other.

In October 2008 I got a phone call, nothing out of the ordinary but just another one of our checkup calls, but this call was a little different because she was no longer with her girlfriend that she was with before and I was broken up with my ex for over 6 months. I was over the hurt and pain from my relationship. I was lonely though! But was not going to jump back into a relationship, just because. We talked and talked more often than normal and sexy mama was smart, very educated, loving, a great friend, passionate, understanding, and a great person over all. I looked past her looks and liked her for her.

The next month I got a call saying that my ex and her current ex were dating. I didn't really care at all because I was over the stalker and I already been in and out another relationship after her with Mute. I wasn't worried about what my ex was doing, really? Sexy mama was very concerned about the whole thing. She would start telling me things that would make me question my kids relationship that they still had with my ex. Sexy mama was really hurt because it was done under her nose and she was played at the end of it all. Sexy mama was in love with her ex and they had a long relationship and friendship and it was all gone when someone took her place.

Not knowing that the phone call in October to me was to get back at them for sexy mama. Make them mad and get them jealous, those were not my attentions at all. I'm not that kind of person anymore. Karma comes back and hits you 10 times harder. I was over all the darn and games and revenge.

Sexy mama and I started off as friends of 3 and half years previous to us being in a relationship. Before we decided to get into a relationship, we took it slow. I never told her that she couldn't talk to her ex or have ties with her children. It was told that I did have a problem, which was not true at all. I wanted her to have that bond with them. We ended up spending every single day together, so we decided to move out of her 1 bedroom and move into my 2 bedroom large apartment. We were so happy that we decided not to tell anyone about our relationship because we knew how the gay world would look at us. We didn't care at all so we ended up making an appearance in a club, after 4 months. I know right an appearance, we felt like celebrities "everyone was pointing, whispering, and talking shit." We didn't care we held hands and noticed no one in the place but us two. We got tired of all the looks and comments so we decided to leave. As we were leaving out, one of my exes that played me felt a certain way about me and sexy mama's relationship and she tried to fight me but sexy mama was not on that at all. We ended up leaving enjoying the rest of our night at home. No one could tell us anything!!!

Then there were the Facebook comments, texts, emails, and phone calls. We were getting so much fame that it wasn't funny. We decided to start over in another state and moved away from the haters. In November 2009 we moved to Georgia and we were so happy that no one could tell us anything. It was a spur of the moment move and no one knew about it either. If this is supposed to happen then let it be.

January 23:
I sometimes wonder why do I deal with so much in my life and can't seem to run away from it. I feel like sometimes that I am stuck in a worthless relationship ... Sometimes I just want to leave and never look back at anything that I have done thus far. I want to go and go until I find my way and where I really want to be in life. I want to start my life over again alone sometimes and what I am writing is just a thought and sometimes what I feel.

Venting Continues:
If I was to win the lottery, I would get out of debt and look into buying a house that I can afford in like California. That's where all my dreams will come true. I would up and take all of my clothes and leave everything behind. I would use my bonus miles from delta sky miles and just rent a car and go. I would also change my name and phone number and go missing. I need at least 100k......
I really need to get my life together and stop thinking about what someone else is going to do because I have to think about me and my life and who else to do that than you.
I want so much for myself and all I need is a new start in life. I need to first start what I haven't finished already. Like my book, in 2013 my book will be finished and published for the world to see that I and not a bad person I have just been through a lot in my life that no one will ever understand only if they walked in my shoes...

Joyce Reed

Dec:

Today I woke up feeling differently about life and what it has to offer me. My year started off really iffy. I was fired from my job that I interned at because I spoke up about a situation that put me in between a rock and a hard place. My boss told me some information that pertained to another employee that was a good friend of mines. It was brought up and I had no choice but to tell the truth about the matter. In doing that it caused me to lose my job on Dec 30th. Then after I left my job me and my friend decided to have a drink at the sports bar by my old house on Roswell Rd. and my car stopped on me in the middle of the intersection. It was embarrassing and I was pissed because I just got the car 3 weeks prior. Then when I got home my mom tells me that she ran into a tree and messed the rental up. This all happened within 6 hours. I sat and thought to myself that it's someone out here in this world that is way worse than I am and I am blessed that I have to things I have. I didn't let my old job get to me nor did I get all upset about my car because at the end of the day I still have a house, car, and food.

Joyce Reed

Jan 3rd:
Everything is going good so far this year. My kids are getting much better and we communicate more with one other. Marquis was always quiet and not very talkative but he is starting to open up a little. Tory the counselor came in to talk with myself and Marquis a little just to hear what has been happening thus far.

Dec 06:
Today I woke up and just feel like everything I had done thus far is for shit, I sometimes sit away from everyone and just think about why me ??? And why is my life so fucked up why are my kids so hard headed and disrespectful and why do I always regret everything that I have done. Can I or will I be able to be that person that cares about everything and everyone feelings and then get fucked in the end or should I be the person I have been and just keep going through life like I don't give a fuck because it seems like when I do it that way my life is a little bit better than before. But while I have an I don't give a fuck attitude then people get hurt along the way. I am so lost in this world that it isn't even funny.
Sometimes I think to myself that my kids will always be who they are, is it punishment for me?

Hurt Used To Live Here

Went South Literally:

It all turned sour when I found out that someone was doing this for all the wrong reasons. I was getting fake messages sent to sexy mama that were reworded and dates had been changed. Someone was making fake FB pages to slander my name. I only knew one person that worked in the computer field. You know who you are!!! I was getting message about her cheating on me while we were 700 miles away. We began to start fighting and arguing a lot and more and more emails started to come. We started to fight like strangers on the street. In front of my children and they started not to like her.

How would you feel, if you saw your mom unhappy, arguing, and fighting all the time? Will you like her mate more or less? I couldn't explain clearly enough to sexy mama at all why my children started to change on her and talk back and not listen. Kids, especially boys will be over protective over their mom no matter what there will be a change when they see mommy sad all the time.

It started to only get worse. We ended up moving into a house and things started off really good in the beginning until I started footing all the bills and providing for everyone in the house. My children started to act up. Was it because I still stayed with the same person that brought me hurt and pain? I was following the same footsteps my mom did. I knew that, but what was I to do 800 miles away from everyone and barely had support. I tried to work it out.

I would vent often feeling different emotions all the time. One day I was blaming myself, my kids, my mom, my relationship, didn't really know who to blame... But these are some of my venting moments:

Joyce Reed

WHAT THE FUCK IS IT?

I am so tired of all this and I wish sometimes GOD would take me out of my misery and take me home away from all of this... But how would my children feel when I am gone? Maybe they will then realize how good of a mother I was trying to be or will they be raised to not care like their mother? All I want for them is to be opposite of me and their fathers. I just wish that I could really go back in time and erase everything that ever happened to me. I really don't want to do this anymore. But GOD says you should be careful for what you ask for but all I want is to be happy and my family be a family, but how because the people that mattered to me the most are gone and I just want someone to help me LORD I am begging you to help me build my family so one day I can at lease feel respected by my own family.

I know you may say that it's an excuse but I have been living with this for 13 years that if my mother would have been the mother she should have been then most of the things in my life, would've happened. If she would have put us first then my brother would have been here. I pray for a better me so I CAN be there for my boys and I can be strong enough to be the mother they need but I always let my inner feelings and self-hatred interfere with what I should and shouldn't do. I know my kids did not want to be and damn sure didn't ask to be here but if my woman hood was never taken from me, Marquis would not have to be raise in this SHIT

HOLE called a world and if Martrel's father would have just left after we were arguing and didn't take that choice away from me then he wouldn't be here either. Who can I blame right now? Me as a mother for keep living day by day knowing that my kids were born by force from a man and that's why I hate men to this day. Someone always took something from me beginning at the age of 11 my father took something from me that I will never get back ever and all I wanted was to not be like my mother and father.

My own fucking father took my innocence from me and made me afraid that if someone was to ever do something to me that keeping quiet would be the best thing for me because no one would care, my father used to do harmful things to us as kids. He used to play Russian roulette with us with a loaded gun and make us rub him from head to toe and at that age I never thought that it wasnt ok because that was my father and I knew that he would never hurt us.

Did I tell NO, because what my father said I found out that he was right..... No one cares......

WHO THE FUCK DO I BLAME IF MY LIFE IS FUCKED UP AND I GO AROUND HURTING EVERYONE THAT TRIES TO LOVE ME AND BE THERE FOR ME???? I GO DAY BY DAY HURTING AND NOT ALLOWING ANYONE INSIDE BECAUSE OF WHAT MY FUCKED UP FAMILY HAS DONE TO ME AS A CHILD.

Joyce Reed

july 12:
Today I feel like something is always coming up in my life and I can't seem to get through an entire year lease ever. But why is he trying to tell me that this is what it's like to struggle so get on your business? Or is the devil really that busy? Whichever it is, I would prefer to go with GOD and start writing more and focus on myself. I can give great advice but can never take my own.

This was my way of releasing without causing confrontation. Sexy mama had a really bad attitude and was right all the time, even when she wasn't.

OMG when it came to her bestie's they did no wrong even though they lied, betrayed her, left her stranded, neglected her. When one of her besties followed her to Georgia, I knew that our relationship was over. This was the bestie that I DID NOT LIKE AT ALL coming to ruin the rest of our relationship we are trying to hold on to. She gave away our furniture that was in our house to help her out, WTF about us over here. My house was like storage for her bestie, I hated every minute of it. She would allow her to come and wash her car off of my water bill that I was paying. I couldn't keep up with all the bills on my own so we ended up losing our house. In our worst of time sexy mama was still lying and cheating with her ex that left her for my ex-girlfriend. She was sending her messages telling her that she loved her still and missed her. It was like a slap in my face, when we needed each other the most she betrayed me. I don't take any shit from anybody

Joyce Reed

that tries to play over me. I felt something would always change and I didn't want to think that she was using me to get back at someone else. Sexy mama has yet again hurt me. Why do I keep going back and accepting it? I was in another state that I knew no one on that level. Another woman was the last thing on my mind when we still needed to find a place to live before we had to move within 45 days, our landlord would not let us re-sign the lease. We looked and couldn't find anything. The day is here, that we are moving our things out of this beautiful home that we worked so hard for. We ended up losing everything we had because we couldn't afford a bigger truck or storage. I ended up being homeless and I ended up coming back to Chicago for 2 months until I got a break. An apartment was going to accept my messed up credit and we ended up moving back to Georgia with a fresh start. Sexy mama ended up coming back with us only for a couple of weeks. We decided that this relationship wasn't healthy and we needed to go our separate ways. After dealing with sexy mama, I was tired I used to pray that GOD show me who I should be with and guide me to my future mate. I have a list that I wrote down of what my ideal person would be and GOD please bring me to them. It being a man or a woman GOD shows me where you want me to be. I was so tired of getting into re-lationships that wasn't healthy for me or my kids. I needed him to give me my soul mate.

Hurt Used To Live Here

Dear Diary:

RIGHT NOW I HAVE THE PERFECT WOMAN IN MY LIFE AND ALL SHE WANTS IS FOR ME TO BE HAPPY AND SHE TRIES HER HARDEST TO DO THAT BUT ME BEING THE FUCKED UP PERSON I AM I CANT ALLOW HER TO BE THE PERSON SHE REALLY IS... I DONT THINK THAT I AM GOOD ENOUGH FOR ANYONE OR ANYTHING. I HAVE BEEN LIVING A LIE TO MYSELF, MY KIDS AND GOD AND ALL I AM DOING IS LETTING HIM DOWN, IF THERE IS A GOD WHERE IS HE BECAUSE I NEED HIM RIGHT NOW TO KEEP MY FAMILY TOGETHER BECAUSE RIGHT NOW AT THIS POINT I WANT TO GIVE UP ON LIFE AND JUST BE WITH WHO I KNOW LOVES ME THE MOST AND THAT'S MY BROTHER, HE WOULD NEVER ALLOW HALF OF THIS SHIT TO GO!

I am so hurt that I cry and don't even know what I'm crying for and this shit hurts a lot to know that one day all of this will be out in the open and it will be too late to fix because I have ended it all because of it...

I hope when everyone reads this they will have a better understanding about me and why I am he way I am and not judge me like they have been all my life.

NOW DO I WANT SELF PITY AND YOU TO FEEL SORRY? NO, ALL I WANT AND HAVE BEEN ASKING FOR IS HELP FROM SOMEONE THAT REALLY LOVES ME. SOMEONE I CAN TRUST NOT TO HOLD THIS AGAINST ME OR USE IT AGAINST ME, I WANT HELP!!
WHY ME?

Joyce Reed

FINAL

Chapter 12

MY CHANGE - MY OUTCOME

"After this day I knew GOD was real, it took all of this to realize that he will NEVER leave you nor forsake you."

One this particular morning, I woke up feeling down like any other day in the past month. Today, everything was just hitting me all at once. I lost my job, I was getting evicted in a couple of days, my phone was off, my cable was off, my car was remotely controlled by a box and since I didn't pay the note, I knew that I only had 48 hours before my car wouldn't start. My kids were getting put out of school because someone told them we had moved out of the area. I have 5 cents to my name, and we had no food. We had gone through yet another loaf of bread and bologna, and all the can goods. I lost 25 pounds and looked like a crack head! My underwear was falling off of my body; my bra couldn't fit, nor the rest of my clothes. I was crying, depressed, and still had no help or support from any of my family. Mind you, I was living hundreds of miles away from my hometown of Chicago.

My mom was the only one that could make me cry and she made sure that she did that. After speaking with her over the phone and her not understanding fully what I was going through, she was very negative, and said: "Well Joyce, Well!!! I told you not to …" "Mom, I need comfort and support and love and a since of knowing that you are still here for me no matter what and that everything will be ok."

Can all this be happening to me at once, AGAIN?

She was so negative about the situation because she felt for her own selfish reasons that we should have never left in the first place and I should have kept the boys there. My mom always wanted to feel needed and wanted for some reason. If I would ask her for anything thing, she would put up a fuss and then eventually give it to me but tell everyone that I am using her and taking her bill money from her. I was always made to look like the bad person all the time.

After hanging up the phone with her and thinking a little bit more I realized that even after 23, my life still feels like I was unwanted and unloved by the ones that are supposed to love you the most. I couldn't count on anyone in my family because they were only worried about their self. I had a sister that had the money to help out and never extended a phone call or a how are you and the boys doing? My sister was never in my life like that or my kid's life. She didn't call for their birthdays or holidays. She was the worst auntie in the world. She was only worried about her and her other side of the family. This was the worst feeling ever to have to need someone but no one was ever anywhere to be found.

GOD IS REAL:

I decided to take 20 pills from 3 different pill bottles. I took everything that was left in my medicine cabinet. This was the second time I tried to commit suicide. Before I did that, I wrote a letter telling my family that I wanted my children to go live with my auntie. I didn't want my children near the woman that tried to turn my kids against me and always talk down about me to them. I laid down in my walk in closet in my bedroom, bald up in the corner, while my children were in the other room and hoped that I would go to sleep and didn't wake up. I didn't care about anything at this time, my body and my soul was completely numb from the world and myself. After laying there for like 30 minutes and looking around in the dark on the floor trying to understand why I couldn't fall asleep. My free government phone would not stop ringing; maybe it's a sign from GOD preventing me from falling asleep? So after an hour of not being able to fall asleep, I grabbed the boys and explained to them that I was tired of living and it was time to end all our lives because I don't want you all to be with anyone but me. Mommy just can't do this anymore and if I take my life, I'm taking your lives as well because no one will take care of you like I will.

It was like something was taking over my body.

I had no feeling or regrets about anything. The boys and I got in the car and I told them that we are about to die. I don't know if they really believed me.

I am about to kill all of us, I told them!

As I am on this two-lane expressway driving really fast in the left lane looking for a place to drive my car off the cliff. After driving like 10 miles, I finally found a deep cliff to run my car off. As I try to get over in the right lane end our life, I could not get over in the right lane at all. There were no cars in front or back of me in the left lane, but everyone drove in the right lane. It was odd to me but it seem like no one would let me over and it was back to back traffic in the right lane but there was no one in the left lane with me at all. It was like I was the only car on that side and the right lane was backed up with bumper to bumper traffic.

Was that another sign from GOD?

When I was finally able to get over to the right of course I passed the cliff already. So my plan was not working for me at all. My kids were screaming and crying because of how fast I was driving and after me cursing and screaming they finally realized that mommy is for real and we are about to die. I still didn't feel remorse nor had any feelings in my body at all. There cries and screams went silent and it felt like someone took over my body in that car. I could see everything that was going on but felt like I was in a different place. I was in a daze for a while because I heard no sound, everything just went silent. As I continue to drive there was an exit that I was forced to get off, like someone opened the expressway for me because right now all the cars were all gone? As I got off there was no left or right turn permitted. I am still driving in anger, and as I drove I see a huge Church, it was the only thing I saw. I pulled in the parking lot and cried for about 15 minutes. I was screaming what have I done, what is going on with me, why am I doing this to my family. After the 15 minutes passed it was cold so we decided to get out of the car and walk in the church. There was no one in site so we walked around lost in the huge church until we ran into a nice lady and she asked us what I was looking for? I told her that I have no clue. She noticed that we all have been crying and in shock and really had a lost look on our face. I was in a daze still and didn't know what I needed at the moment. She said come with me.

Do you mind if I separate you from the boys?

I am going to take them to the teen center and you are going with me.

I told her yeah, sure. Go ahead.

Hurt Used To Live Here

She then guided to a room and my children were guided to another room for their age group. When I walked I walked into the room, it was like everyone eyes were on me and it felt like they knew what had just happened to me 2 hours ago. It was so weird. I already look like I was homeless because I had on some oversized jogging pants and a big oversized shirt because none of my clothes fit anyway. The only thing I had on me was a purse that nothing of value was in it. I found me a sit in the back of the room and the person that was talking just interrupted his sermon and said let's say a prayer. As we bowed our head and I listened in prayer, it felt like he was praying just for me and I felt a chill run through my body. My eyes are cloed the whole time and im just thanking GOD that he was on my side and he lead me to this church to save me. When it was time to say Amen, I opened my eyes and people just start walking up to me hugging me and holding me. I just bursted out in tears and kept saying thank you, thank you over and over again.

This one lady that I was talking to I told her what had happened that day and what I was forced with and we both cried together. She said that GOD will make sure he finds a way for you and your family. After all the crying, I had to go to the bathroom and clean up my face. I felt like I was in a safe place so I decided to leave my purse on the seat while I went to the bathroom. I was gone for like 15-20 minutes. When I returned people was handing me money and gift cards from everywhere. I just fell to my knees and praised GOD. I don't know if I was catching the Holy Ghost but whatever it was a powerful force that came through me. I had to sit down for a minute and catch my breath and take all this in for a second because all I'm thinking about is how Blessed I am right now and how GOD works. I'm so glad that GOD led me this this church.

Me and my children stayed at the church for 4 hours that day and after leaving I felt like a new person. I didn't have doubt. I had no worries. I had a new outlook on life and gained a new support team that really had my back. Me and the boys went home. I didn't even worry about us getting evicted in a couple of days because I knew that he already had a plan for my life. I knew that he would not bring me this far to leave me like this.

After that night we went home with a different outlook on life itself. I was relaxed, and I know that will never leave you or forsake me. I grabbed my purse and found $320.00 in cash in it there were $5 to $20 bills throughout my purse. Right then is when I knew that GOD IS REAL – HE HAS A PLAN FOR ME, and ending it was not a part of his plan!!!!

Me and the boys walked to McDonalds nearby and got us a 20 piece nugget and 3 fries and apple pies and sat in the car and ate it because we have been living off of bread and can goods. That meal taste like a thanksgiving dinner. It was amazing and just to see them smile melted my heart. We went home and I went to sleep with a sound mind and I hugged and kissed my boys and told them that I was so sorry for all of this and it will never happen again. My kids were so loving and caring. They just gave me a hug and we all slept together on the floor in the livingroom. I wanted them to know that I was there for them and I loved them until my heart stopped beating.

Over the years I have learned that GOD has brought me through such tragic experiences so that I would be able to share my stories to not only help me, but to help other abused, neglected, hurt, single mothers, teen mothers and victims. By sharing my story you would have been able to relate on some type of level and knowing that you are not alone is somewhat of a healing process for me.

Women, you are worth more than your clothes, your red bottoms that pole your legs, your $2000.00 purse. You are worth more than that; you are worth RESPECT, LOVE and HONESTY. Never settle for what looks good because what looks good is not always good. I had to learn that the hard and painful way. I created a list for who I wanted to spend the rest of my life with and if you are off one thing that is on my list that is considered settling for less. Stick to your list and stay strong with it. People will take you there and there and try you but you know what your worth and until you find that person that will give you all you want it will be like a roller-coaster until you will be hanging upside down and stuck in the air. Just don't settle and you know you are worth more than what they are giving you? Until then I'll just stick to daydreaming and fantasizing about my mate. I think about all my exes and if I could take at least one thing from them all, I would have a perfect mate. That's just a thought that I have from time to time and then I wake up and say to myself that they are all ex's for a reason. But I'm patient!

My Opinion:

I never ever wanted to get married. If you would have asked me five years ago about marriage. I would have told you what I have been saying all my life; "HELL NAW!!" If you want to marry, we can type up a letter/agreement and sign the bottom and take it to the nearest currency exchange and get it notarized for $1.50 as opposed to spending thousands of dollars on dresses, invitations, plates, and gas and time , and then spending thousands more to get a divorce. We can go the simple route and just buy rings and pay $1.50 for the notary and when we want out, we just rip the letter up and go our separate ways. I know have a different look on life and what I want my life to be.

If:

I think if I had to change anything in my life, it wouldn't be to rewind my life and change it, or to have a new family or to have stayed in school. It wouldn't been to even better mom than I am now to my boys. If I knew then what I know now, then I would have been there from day one with both of my children and to have given them all of my love and attention that they were missing at an early age and never used excuses. Children are so precious and helpless. They didn't ask to be here no matter what the circumstances are or was. Do what you have to do to raise your children and love them and hold them read to them, sing to them, teach them right from wrong and just be there for them and give them what you didn't have. If that's just a hug, or love, or even a kiss ... give it to them; they know when they are loved. You can see it in their big smile.

I allowed my anger and disappointments from others to interfere with the relationship I should have had with my boys. Now, I know that you can't allow someone else's actions or reactions cause you to act out on anyone, especially someone you love. I learned and I am still learning that being loud, disrespectful, rude, and hurtful will not do anything but hurt you in the long run. If bursting a blood vessel, or smacking the shit out of someone and accidentally hitting them in the teeth with your knuckle, or even saying things that you will later regret, just walk away. I don't like being angry! I also realized that in my life as a young girl I was looking for love in all the wrong places and all from the wrong people. I lived a very interesting life and I wouldn't change it for anything in the world. GOD choose me and he choose me because he knew I could handle anything that was thrown my way and now I have to give back and live my purpose.

My Worth:

I am at a point in my life where I want to settle down and be happy and finish raising my kids in a healthier environment. As they say it takes a village to raise a child and I say it takes a MAN to raise a boy to become a MAN! No matter what, boys don't want to have that talk with their mom or to talk about girls. I can tell them to raise the toilet seat and why, but a man can tell them what's real and explain all the feelings and emotions that they are going through. I can tell them how to protect themselves but a man can tell them what to expect. There's only so much a woman can do. I'm not saying they can't be great leaders and a man themselves but there is nothing like getting and giving advice from a man's perspective. Even if it is a male role model, a man needs to be involved in their life at some point.

After my last female relationship that ended in 2010 with "sexy mama" it left me convinced that a woman is just not for me. I've been dealing with women since 2000 and there were definitely great times, but then there were bad times. Arguing, fighting, jealous rages, gossip, DRAMA, and a bunch of messy chicks with emotional problems. Even though I have experienced painful, unfulfilling boring or just whack ass sex from a man, I think it is time to give it a real try. Or just let him lead me to the right one. I have my list and GOD knows what I need and I'm just waiting for

"Mr. Right" to come scoop me up.

It blew my mind when my youngest turned to me as I'm sitting on my bed and he turns to me and said; "Mom, when are you going to get a man because from the looks of it you are going to be single forever?" I said" Boy how do you know that?" He responded by saying;

"Mommy, you been single for two years now." I said damn! Kids know just what to say.

He cleans it up by saying;

"Well. I just want you to be happy because you deserve it I love you Mommy."

He leans over and hugs me and kisses me on the cheek.

Let In:

There are some things that I need to work on and they are trusting and letting people in and not thinking that they are out to get me. By me being on my own since I was 16, living in my own apartment and taking care of everything on my own, it's kind of hard to allow someone to come in and take over. That's why I am working on it, allowing someone in my world, I was always scared to let them all the way in because I have shared personal stories with people and they used them against me or threw them in my face later. I want the next time to be the last time and if I have to continue to buy "batteries" for the next 2 years then so be it. I am only getting older not younger!!

Words of Wisdom:

I want to share some words of wisdom and encouragement that has helped me in rough times and different situations. Life is bigger than you!! You are here on this earth for a reason.

These are NOT my words:

God said:

Hi!

As you got up this morning, I watched you and hoped you would talk to me, even if it was just a few words, asking my opinion or thanking me for something good that happened in your life yesterday – but I noticed you were too busy trying to find the outfit to put on and wear to work.

I waited again. When you ran around the house getting ready I knew there would be a few minutes for you to stop and say hello, but you were too busy. At one point you had to wait fifteen minutes with nothing to do but sit in a chair. Then I saw you spring to your feet. I thought you wanted to talk to me but you ran to the phone and called a friend to get the latest gossip.

I watched you as you went to work and waited patiently all day long. With all your activities I guess you were too busy to say anything to me. I noticed that before lunch you looked around, maybe you felt embarrassed to talk to me that is why you didn't bow your head. You glanced three or four over and noticed some of your friends talking to me briefly before they ate, but you didn't. That's okay. There is still more time left, and I have to hope that you will talk to me, yet you went home and it seems as if you had lots of things to do. After a few of them were done you turned on your TV. I don't know if you like TV or not, just about anything goes on there and you spend a lot of time each day in front of it, not thinking about anything – just enjoying the show. I *waited patiently again as you watched TV and ate your meal but again you didn't talk to me. Bedtime....I guess you felt tired. After you said goodnight to your family you plopped into and fell asleep in no time. That's okay because you may not realize that I am always there for you. I've got patience more than you will ever know. I even want to teach you how to be patient with others as well.*

I love you so much that I waited every day for a nod, a prayer or thought or a thankful part of your heart. It is hard to have a one-sided conversation. Well, you are getting up again and once again I will wait with nothing but love for you hoping that today you will give me some time. Have a nice day!

Your friend,
GOD
"Un-Known Author"

This letter is so special to me and just thinking about it brought tears to my eyes, hear goes… This is for the fellas that think they know a woman.. If they did they would be gentler with us.

WHY Woman Cry:

A little boy asked his mother, "Why are you crying?" "Because I'm a woman", She told him.

"I don't understand," he said. His Mom just hugged him and said, 'And you never will.

Later the little boy asked his father, 'Why does Mother seem to cry for no reason?

All woman cry for no reason, was all his dad could say.

The little boy grew up and became a man, still wondering why women cry.

Finally he put in a call to God. When God got on the phone he asked, 'God, why do women cry easily?'

God said:

'When I made the woman she had to be special.'

'I made her shoulders strong enough to carry the weight of the world, yet gentle enough to give comfort.'

'I gave her an inner strength to endure childbirth and the rejection that many times comes from her children.'

'I gave her hardness that allows her to keep going when everyone else gives up, and take care of her family through sickness and fatigue without complaining.'

'I gave her the sensitivity to love her children under and all circumstances, even when her child has hurt her very badly.'

'And finally, I gave her a tear to shed.' 'This hers exclusively to use whenever it is needed.'

'That tear holds more than men could understand.'

'If a man was to shed her tear it would look enormous.'

'For a woman's tear is full of unconditional love, power, sacrifice, beauty, pain and compassion.'

'All tenfold of what a Man is able to feel.'

'And that my son is, why I made her I made her as close to is Supernatural.'

'She's my gift to the world she's an Angel on Earth.' "Love her and praise her for there will be no other here on Earth that will Love you like I do than your Mother.'

'You see my son,' said God, 'The beauty of a woman is not in the clothes she wears, the figure that she carries, or the way she combs her hair.'

The beauty of a woman must be seen in her eyes, because that is the doorway to her heart- the place where love resides.'

Joyce Reed

"Un-Known Author"

These words have helped me through depressing moments, crying moments, and or happy moments. If it helped me then I know it would help you as well.

By writing this book it has changed my life in so many different ways in life. I have learned how to be patient with people and try to maintain a positive attitude.

Ignorance is taught not learned.

This is what I posted on my refrigerator just to remind me of how important it is to thank the man upstairs for all that he has done for you thank him for all that you have and everything else will follow. I was told that if everyone had to put all their problems in a pile, you would be the first to grab yours right back out of that pile. Don't complain of what you don't have but be blessed for what you do have!

My boys are the most important to me in this world and without them I would not be the woman I am today. I know that I did wrong and made some bad choices in life but just understand that I was young and didn't mean to hurt you guys in any way, speaking to my sons. If I subjected you all to violence in your lives, mommy is sorry, again speaking to my sons. I never want you guys to not feel loved and feel like you are being raised alone. I am behind you guys until we part this earth until then I will do what I can to give you the best life possible.

I have been through hell and back in my life and it has not stopped me once. I may have had some bad times or downfalls, but I got right back up. Even after writing this in my journal I found out GOD was real and He is not done with me yet! Until then live by Him and He will see you through it. He brought me through it for a reason not to break me but to build me up. The devil just used some people to harm me. GOD installed power within me so that I can survive it. I did it, now it's time to help others use that same strength.

My Motto:
Give without expecting anything in return.
Love like tomorrow isn't promised.
Live today, like it's your last.

Deuteronomy 31:6
"Be strong and courageous. Do not be afraid or terrified because of them, for the Lord your God goes with you; He will never leave you or forsake you." This has gotten me through a lot of hard times. If it helped me, I know that it will help you

Dear mommy,

I want you to know that most of my life has been a blur because I had to block out all of the negativity that has happened to me. When I was growing up, I blamed you for a lot because I thought that since my dad wasn't there to protect me, you would be the person to protect me and guide me through life. There are things that I didn't agree with that you did in the past but I have lived, learned and forgave you for everything that has happened in my life.

I hope by you reading this book you take all the good out of it and take my words as a little girl is talking and love me for who I was and also who I turned out to be. I hope you have a better understanding on what my life was like growing up alone. Even though you were there financially I wish you were there for everything else.

I know that everything changed when you lost your granny, your mother, your father and your son in the same year and I know it affected you because you were never the same after that. I can't tell you enough that I forgive you for everything that was out of your control. We are now in a better place and I want us to continue to grow together.

I love you
Sincerely,
Your baby girl

Hurt Used To Live Here

A letter from my boys

Dear Mom,
Congratulations, you are finally done with your book. I'm so proud of you, I know we didn't have much growing up as much as you wished, somehow you made it work, you are a strong beautiful woman. Dreams are finally coming true and accomplishments are finally being accomplished.
I wish you the best
I LOVE YOU
Marquis

You are beautiful, intelligent, and strong. You always make me smile when I look at your eyes and see you happy. I am happy to have you as a mom; I will try my best to make you smile, always. I will never forget all the fun times and talks we have about life. All I really want from you is promise to never take my hugs away.
Keep it up mom
I love you
Martrel

Question & Topics for Discussion

1. Can you benefit or relate from what you read?

2. How do you get pass betrayal?

3. What does LOVE mean to you?

4. Do you ever regret something in life you did?

5. When do you know you had enough?

6. What defines a REAL man/woman?

7. When you say these words, what is the first two words that come to mind?

-Trust
-Respect
-Struggle
-Pain
-Lonely

8. Is there something that you have learned or were inspired by reading?

Coming 2016

Speechless NO more!

Somewhere behind all that HURT and PAIN, lies a voice that helped, inspired and motivated others. Her voice was always un-heard or covered by a smile that really held so much HURT and PAIN behind it.

What you see now is a woman that made it through the storm and jumped over every hurdle and ran through each obstacle and came out a winner and a voice for many.

She was that lost little girl that found her VOICE and NEVER looked back at what made her that bitter and anger soul.
She now stands before you a woman of many things.

She never thought that she would make it out alive but she did, just by having faith in GOD and speaking out and never being ashamed of what she has been though.

It's Her LIFE, Her JOURNEY and Her STRUGGLE, that made her the woman she is today.

It's NOT your fault!! Speak out and be HEARD!
Speechless NO more!

I AM that girl with a VOICE!!

Author Joyce Reed
www.iamURvoice.com